QUESTIONS & ANSWERS:
Remedies

Multiple Choice and Short Answer

By

RACHEL M. JANUTIS
Associate Professor of Law
Capital University Law School

TRACY A. THOMAS
Professor of Law and Director of Faculty Research and Development
University of Akron School of Law

CAROLINA ACADEMIC PRESS
Durham, North Carolina

ISBN#: 0820570788

Carolina Academic Press, LLC
700 Kent Street
Durham, North Carolina 27701
Telephone (919) 489-7486
Fax (919) 493-5668
www.caplaw.com

Printed in the United States of America

ABOUT THE AUTHORS

Rachel M. Janutis is Associate Professor of Law at Capital University Law School. She teaches courses in Remedies, Civil Procedure and Complex Litigation. Before she began teaching, Professor Janutis practiced as a commercial litigator for several years, and she also clerked for a federal judge. Professor Janutis is a co-author with Professors Elaine Shoben and Murray Tabb of CASES AND PROBLEMS ON REMEDIES. She also has authored several articles on remedies and civil procedure. She is a member of the United States Supreme Court Bar, the State Bar of Illinois, the American Bar Association, the Illinois State Bar Association, the Ohio State Bar Association and the Columbus Bar Association. Professor Janutis previously served on the executive committee of the Remedies section of the American Association of Law Schools.

Tracy A. Thomas is Professor of Law and Director of Faculty Research and Development at the University of Akron School of Law. Her teaching interests include Remedies, Family Law, and Women's Legal History. Prior to teaching, Professor Thomas was a litigator in Washington, D.C. and a clerk for a federal appellate judge. She has written numerous law review articles on remedies and the Constitution and the U.S. Supreme Court and remedies, and is a co-editor of the casebook, REMEDIES: PUBLIC AND PRIVATE. She previously served on the executive committee of the Remedies section of the Association of American Law Schools. She is a member of the United States Supreme Court Bar, the State Bar of California, the District of Columbia Bar, and the Ohio State Bar Association.

PREFACE

Most courses in law school focus on one substantive area of law — tort law or contract law — and explore how that body of law applies to various factual settings. The study of Remedies provides students with a unique opportunity to study the law from a trans-substantive perspective. By integrating the various substantive areas of law, Remedies allows students to focus on the commonalities of judicial relief across the board. In Remedies, students also consider how legal theories from several substantive areas of law can apply to a single transaction or dispute and how those differing legal theories may produce different outcomes in a given case. Remedies also provides students with an opportunity to observe how the law impacts the everyday lives of the parties to litigation by focusing on what relief the parties will take from the case — the "bottom line." Finally, through the study of Remedies, students can gain insight into the value that society places on various personal rights and interests. Remedies explores questions about which losses we choose to compensate as well as the manner in which we compensate and value those losses. The answers to these questions reflect on the value we place on the underlying rights and interests that have been harmed.

This book is designed to guide students through the study of this multi-faceted area of the law. It can be used to assist in preparation for a final exam. However, students will also find it useful to assist in understanding core topics and issues during the course of the semester.

To this end, the first part of the book is divided into separate chapters. Each chapter concerns one specific Remedies topic. The topics covered in these chapters represent the core topics covered by most leading Remedies casebooks. Each of these chapters provides multiple choice and short answer questions covering the main issues surrounding the specified topic. The questions are designed to highlight common areas of misunderstanding. The corresponding answers and explanations are intended to dispel common misconceptions and strengthen understanding and comprehension of troublesome areas.

The second part of the book consists of a practice final exam. The practice final exam, like the individual chapters, consists of multiple choice and short answer questions. However, unlike the first part of the book, the topic or topics covered by a question are not expressly identified. Additionally, the questions are not organized by topic but rather appear in a randomly selected order. Finally, some of the questions raise issues pertaining to multiple topics.

We hope that students will find this book to be useful and that students will find the study of Remedies to be both fascinating and thought-provoking. Finally, we wish to thank Soni Schuman for her invaluable assistance in helping us prepare the manuscript and our families for their support and patience during the completion of this project.

Rachel M. Janutis
Tracy A. Thomas
January 2007

TABLE OF CONTENTS

QUESTIONS

1. Which of the following are remedies at law?

   (A) Replevin.

   (B) Specific Performance.

   (C) Constructive Trust.

   (D) Backpay.

2. What is the difference between substitutional and specific remedies?

ANSWER:

3. Plaintiff, a former employee, sued Employer, alleging that Employer wrongfully fired Plaintiff for engaging in political conduct. Plaintiff initially sought reinstatement and backpay. Plaintiff filed an amended complaint, seeking front pay in lieu of reinstatement and adding a jury demand. Employer moved to strike Plaintiff's jury demand. Assuming that Plaintiff's jury demand is timely, how should the court rule on Employer's motion?

   (A) The court should grant the motion because Plaintiff seeks both legal and equitable relief.

   (B) The court should grant the motion because Plaintiff seeks only equitable relief.

   (C) The court should deny the motion because Plaintiff seeks only monetary relief.

   (D) The court should deny the motion because Plaintiff seeks both legal and equitable relief.

4. Calibraska state law makes it illegal for an employer to inquire into an employee's credit history or perform a credit check on an employee as a condition of employment. The statute provides that:

   > An employee who is aggrieved by a violation of this Act is entitled to recover from the violating employer $500 per violation and attorney fees incurred in maintaining an action against the employer.

   Until recently, Potter was employed by Darko Industries in its Calibraska office. Unbeknownst to Potter, a Darko supervisor obtained a copy of Potter's credit report from a consumer reporting agency. As a result of the information contained in the credit report, Darko fired Potter. Despite reasonable efforts, Potter has been unable to find another job. Potter brought an action against Darko under the statute. In the lawsuit, Potter seeks reinstatement and backpay. Assuming that Potter can show that Darko violated the Act, what are the best arguments in favor of granting Potter reinstatement and backpay? What are the best arguments in favor of limiting Potter's recovery to $500 and attorneys fees?

ANSWER:

5. Contractor entered into a contract to construct an office building according to Owner's specifications. The specifications called for the front door of the building to face south. Contractor constructed the building with the door facing west. Owner sued Contractor for breach of contract. Under which of the following circumstances, if any, is Owner likely to recover the cost to remedy the error?

(A) The building must be razed and rebuilt with the front door facing south.

(B) A building with a front door facing south is more aesthetically pleasing than a building with a front door facing west.

(C) The specifications called for the front door to face south so that Owner could capitalize on prevailing winds to cool the building.

(D) Owner will not be entitled to recover the cost to remedy the defect under any circumstances.

6. After retiring from a successful career as an attorney, Benson entered into an agreement to open and operate a Pizza Pal franchise restaurant. Under the terms of the franchise agreement, Pizza Pal agreed to permit Benson to use its trademarks and name. Pizza Pal also agreed to provide Benson with its secret recipe. In exchange, Benson agreed to use reasonable efforts to promote the franchise and to pay Pizza Pal a certain percentage of the profits. Benson spent $10,000 to advertise the opening of the franchise. Two days before the mutually agreed upon opening date, Pizza Pal repudiated the contract. If Benson sues Pizza Pal for breach of contract, what will be the likely measure of Benson's recovery?

(A) Benson will be entitled to recover lost profits because Benson's success as an attorney demonstrates that Benson would have operated a successful franchise.

(B) Benson will be entitled to recover the money expended to advertise the restaurant because Benson expended the money in essential reliance under the contract.

(C) Benson will be entitled to recover both the lost profits and the money expended on advertising.

(D) Benson will be entitled to no damages because Benson cannot prove any losses with reasonable certainty.

7. Which of the following is not an example of special or consequential damages?

(A) Medical expenses in a personal injury action.

(B) Damages for lost use in an action for damage to an automobile.

(C)   Lost earnings in an action for defamation.

(D)   None of the above.

8.   Under which of the following circumstances will the buyer be most likely to recover lost profits?

(A)   A finished goods manufacturer produces contracted-for component parts in-house at a cost that exceeds the market value of substitute component parts.

(B)   A sole proprietor fails to purchase a replacement delivery truck when a comparable truck is available at the same price in a different state.

(C)   A farmer is unable to find a replacement tractor at the start of the planting season when the seller repudiated the contract three months before the start of the planting season.

(D)   None of the above.

9.   Distinguish conduct which constitutes comparative or contributory negligence from conduct which constitutes a failure to mitigate damages.

ANSWER:

10. Parker bought a used car from Fast Eddie's Used Car Lot. The Fast Eddie's sales person represented that the car had been driven for fewer than 3000 miles. In reality, the car had been driven for more than 5000 miles. If Parker brings a fraud action against Fast Eddie's, which of the following will be true?

(A)   Parker will not be entitled to pre-judgment interest because Parker is bringing a tort claim.

(B)   Parker will be entitled to pre-judgment interest only if Fast Eddie's concedes liability.

(C)   Parker will be entitled to pre-judgment interest only if Parker's damages are determined by the difference in fair market value between the car as represented and the car as delivered.

(D)   Parker will be entitled to pre-judgment interest under any circumstances.

11. Potter and Davis got into a fight in a bar. Potter suffered serious injuries in the fight. Potter sued Davis for battery. If Potter seeks damages for pain and suffering as well as medical expenses in the lawsuit, which of the following is true?

(A)   Potter will not be entitled to post-judgment interest because Potter is bringing a tort claim.

(B) Potter will not be entitled to post-judgment interest on any damages for pain and suffering because pain and suffering damages are committed to the discretion of the jury.

(C) Potter will be entitled to post-judgment interest only if Davis concedes liability.

(D) Potter will be entitled to post-judgment interest under any circumstances.

12. Buyer and Seller entered into a contract for the sale of 5000 widgets at a price of $1.00 per widget. At the time and place for delivery, Seller delivered only 3000 widgets. Buyer paid Seller for the 3000 widgets. Buyer did not seek to obtain substitute widgets. The fair market price of widgets at the time and place for delivery was $4.00 per widget. In an action for breach of contract, Buyer will be entitled to recover which of the following?

   (A) $2000.

   (B) $6000.

   (C) $8000.

   (D) Buyer will not be entitled to recover damages because Buyer did not make reasonable efforts to cover.

13. Bombay Bicycle Company and Super Sprockets Inc. entered into a contract for the sale of 10,000 sprocket wheels. Bombay agreed to pay $1.00 per wheel for a total of $10,000. Unbeknownst to Super Sprockets, Bombay intended to install the sprocket wheels as component parts on Bombay's finished bicycles. Super Sprockets delivered to Bombay 10,000 bicycle sprocket wheels. However, the sprocket wheels were not the size called for in the contract specifications and did not fit in Bombay's finished bikes. Bombay rejected the sprocket wheels, then purchased 10,000 replacement sprocket wheels from Sprockets International. The replacement sprocket wheels conformed to the specifications under the original contract. Bombay paid Sprockets International $3.00 per wheel. In an action for breach of contract, Bombay will be entitled to recover which of the following?

   (A) $20,000.

   (B) $30,000.

   (C) Bombay will not be entitled to recover damages. Because the replacement sprocket wheels cost more than the original sprocket wheels, they were not commercially reasonable substitute goods.

   (D) Bombay will not be entitled to recover damages because Bombay did not inform Super Sprockets at the time of contracting of Bombay's intent to use the sprocket wheels in finished bicycles.

14. Betty contracted to purchase a used van from Stan for $10,000. At the time and place for delivery, Stan informed Betty that he would not sell the van to Betty. Betty protested that she needed the van so that she could open her delivery business. Stan refused again to sell the van. Betty searched for a comparable van, but none was available. In an action for breach of contract, which of the following is true?

   (A) Betty will be entitled to recover any lost profits from the operation of her delivery business, because the lost profits were foreseeable at the time of the breach and Betty's lost profits were unavoidable.

   (B) Betty will not be entitled to recover her lost profits even though they were unavoidable, because Betty's lost profits were not foreseeable at the time of contracting.

   (C) Betty will not be entitled to recover her lost profits even though they were foreseeable at the time of breach, because she did not mitigate her damages by purchasing a comparable van.

   (D) Betty will not be entitled to recover her lost profits because her lost profits were not foreseeable at the time of contracting and because Betty failed to mitigate her damages.

15. Electric Company entered into a contract to manufacturer and install an electric transformer for Metals Company. The contract contained a clause excluding recovery for consequential damages. Electric Company delivered a conforming transformer but improperly installed the transformer, causing extensive harm to the transformer. In an action for breach of contract by Metals Company, what will be the proper measure of recovery?

   (A) Metals Company will be entitled to recover the cost to repair the transformer.

   (B) Metals Company will be entitled to recover the lesser of the cost to repair the transformer or the diminution in the fair market value of the transformer.

   (C) Metals Company will be entitled to recover the difference in value between the installation service as contracted for and the installation service as received.

   (D) Metals Company will be entitled to recover both the difference in value in the installation service and lesser of the cost to repair or the diminution in value.

16. Simon agreed to sell Barbara 500,000 bricks at a price of $0.10 per brick. At the time and place for delivery, Barbara accepted only 300,000 bricks and wrongfully rejected the remaining 200,000. At the time and place for delivery, the market price of the bricks

was $0.08 per brick. If Simon does not resell the remaining 200,000 bricks, what will be the measure of his damages?

ANSWER:

Questions 17–18 are based on the following fact pattern.

Stone agreed to sell Brown 5,000 Valentine's Day theme greeting cards for retail sale at a price of $2.00 per card. The contract called for delivery on January 27, Y01. When Stone attempted to deliver the greeting cards, Brown wrongfully rejected them. From January 27, Y01 until February 14, Y01, Stone attempted to find another buyer for the cards but was unable to do so. Stone stored the greeting cards until January 15, Y02 at which time Stone again sought out another buyer. On January 15, Y02, Stone notified Brown that Stone intended to sell the greeting cards to Thomas for $1.00 per card.

17. In an action by Stone against Brown, what will be the likely measure of Stone's damages?

   (A)   Stone will be entitled to recover the contract price of $2.00 per card because the goods were not capable of immediate resale.

   (B)   Stone will be entitled to recover the difference between the resale price of $1.00 per card and the original contract price of $2.00 per card because Stone resold the goods in a commercially reasonable manner.

   (C)   Stone will not be entitled to recover the difference between the contract price and the resale price because Stone unreasonably waited for 1 year to resell the greeting cards.

   (D)   Stone will not be entitled to recover the difference between the resale price and the contract price because Stone resold the greeting cards at a private sale.

18. Stone rented the storage space where the greeting cards were stored. Stone paid $500 to rent the space for the year. Will Stone be entitled to recover the rental fee from Brown?

   (A)   Stone will be entitled to recover the fee because Stone reasonably incurred the fee in attempting to mitigate the loss.

   (B)   Stone will be entitled to recover the fee only because Stone was successful in reselling the greeting cards.

   (C)   Stone will not be entitled to recover the fee because sellers are precluded from recovering consequential damages under the Uniform Commercial Code (UCC).

   (D)   Stone will not be entitled to recover the fee because Stone did not inform Brown that Stone intended to store the greeting cards.

19. Big City Bakery ordered 50 laptop computers from Super Computers, Inc., a successful computer manufacturer. Big City Bakery agreed to purchase the 50 laptop computers at Super Computers' standard retail price. A month before the laptop computers were to be delivered, Big City Bakery cancelled its order. Super Computers resold the 50 laptops to New City Bakery. New City Bakery paid the same standard retail price. In an action for breach of contract against Big City Bakery, what will be the measure of Super Computers' damages?

   (A)   Super Computers will only be able to recover damages if the standard retail price is greater than the fair market value of the laptop computers.

   (B)   Super Computers will not be entitled to recover damages because the resale price is equal to the contract price.

   (C)   Super Computers will be entitled to recover the profit it had expected to make on the sale of the laptop computers to Big City Bakery.

   (D)   Super Computers will be entitled to recover the price of the laptop computers.

20. Buyer entered into a contract with Seller to purchase a specially designed molding machine. The contract provided that Seller was to ship the molding machine via railroad to Buyer's manufacturing plant. In an action for breach of contract by Seller against Buyer, under which of the following circumstances will Seller be entitled to recover the contract price?

   (A)   Buyer wrongfully refuses to accept delivery of the molding machine and Seller is not able to resell the molding machine because it is designed for Buyer's specific uses.

   (B)   Buyer accepts delivery of the molding machine but refuses to pay for the molding machine.

   (C)   The molding machine is stolen from a railroad freight yard after Seller delivers the molding machine to the railroad and makes a contract for its shipment to Buyer.

   (D)   All of the above.

21. Benny's Best Ice Cream Producer entered into a contract with Super Salty's Nut Shoppe to purchase 500 pounds of processed nuts at a price of $5.00 per pound. Super Salty was to process the nuts according to Benny's unique secret recipe for use in Benny's new "nutty surprise" ice cream. Super Salty purchased 500 pounds of unprocessed nuts at a cost of $2.00 per pound. Super Salty also purchased the additional ingredients necessary to process the first 100 pounds of the nuts at a cost of $0.50 per pound. Super Salty estimated that the depreciation of its equipment and rent on its plant would cost $0.50 per pound. Super Salty completed and attempted to deliver 100 pounds of processed nuts to Benny's Best. However, Benny's Best rejected the 100 pounds of completed nuts

and informed Super Salty that it was repudiating the contract because the nutty surprise ice cream had not been well received in consumer taste tests. Super Salty immediately halted processing of the nuts and was able to sell the remaining 400 pounds of unprocessed nuts for $1.00 per pound. Super Salty was unable to resell the 100 pounds of processed nuts. What will be the measure of Super Salty's recovery in an action for breach of contract against Benny's Best?

ANSWER:

22. Which of the following liquidated damage clauses is most likely to be upheld by a court?

    (A) A contract between Shipper and Merchant provides that Merchant agrees to ship a minimum quantity of goods within 3 years and that if Merchant fails to ship the minimum quantity of goods within 3 years, Merchant will pay the difference between the full contract price and the price paid for goods already shipped.

    (B) A lease for a term of years between Landlord and Tenant requires Tenant to pay the present value of all remaining rent due under the lease if Tenant vacates before the lease expires.

    (C) A contract between Contractor and School District specifies that Contractor will complete construction of a new school building by the start of the fall semester and provides that Contractor will pay the fair market monthly rental value for each month that performance is delayed.

    (D) An employment contract between Chief Executive Officer and Corporation expressly designates as an enforceable liquidated damages clause a provision that provides that Chief Executive Officer will pay Corporation an amount equal to the number of years remaining on her contract multiplied by her annual salary if Chief Executive Officer leaves before her contract expires.

23. Brown entered into a contract to purchase a condominium from Smith for $150,000 and paid Smith $15,000 as a down payment. The contract expressly provided that if Brown breached the contract, Smith would retain the $15,000 down payment as payment for the damages occasioned by Brown's breach. Before the closing date, Brown decided not to purchase the condominium and instead purchased a different condominium. Smith refused to return the down payment. In an action by Brown to recover the down payment, which of the following are true?

    (A) Brown will not be entitled to restitution of the down payment because a breaching party cannot maintain an action for restitution.

(B)   Brown will not be entitled to restitution of the down payment because Brown willfully breached the contract.

(C)   Brown will be entitled to restitution of the down payment if Brown can show that Smith could have resold the condominium for $175,000 at the time that Brown breached the contract.

(D)   Brown will be entitled to restitution of the down payment because down payment forfeiture clauses are per se illegal penalty clauses.

24.   Baker entered into a contract to purchase a house from Stone for $300,000. A title search revealed that a utility company has an easement through Stone's garage. As a result, Stone failed to deliver marketable title at the closing. In a breach of contract action by Baker, which of the following are true?

(A)   Baker's recovery may be limited to restitution of any purchase price paid if Stone was unaware of the easement.

(B)   Baker's recovery will not be limited to restitution of any purchase price paid even if Stone was unaware of the easement.

(C)   Baker's recovery will be limited to restitution of any purchase price paid even if Stone was aware of the easement but failed to disclose it.

(D)   Baker will be entitled to recover the profit that Stone would have made on the sale to Baker if Stone was aware of the easement but failed to disclose it.

25.   Biggs entered into a contract to purchase a house from Stanton for $350,000. Biggs paid Stanton $35,000 in earnest money. Biggs intended to pay another $35,000 in cash at the closing. Biggs arranged for a 30-year loan secured by a mortgage on the house for the remaining $280,000. The interest rate on the loan was 6%. A day before the closing, Thompson offered to purchase the home from Stanton for $370,000. Stanton repudiated the contract with Biggs. A month later, Biggs purchased a comparable home for $340,000. Biggs paid $70,000 in cash and obtained a 30-year loan secured by a mortgage for the remaining $270,000. The interest rate on the second loan was 7.5%. In an action for breach of contract by Biggs, what will be the measure of Biggs' damages?

(A)   Biggs has no damages because Biggs purchased a comparable home for less money.

(B)   Biggs is entitled to a return of the $35,000 earnest money only.

(C)   Biggs is entitled to a return of the $35,000 earnest money and the value of interest on $270,000 over 30 years at 1.5% reduced to present value.

(D)   Biggs is entitled to a return of the $35,000 earnest money and the difference between the value of a 30-year $280,000 loan at 6% and a 30-year $270,000 at 7.5% reduced to present value.

26. Penny suffered a broken leg in an auto accident in which Dan was at fault. Dr. Quinn examined, set and cast Penny's leg. After treatment was completed, Dr. Quinn tendered a bill for $5,000. Under which of the following circumstances will Penny be entitled to recover $5,000 from Dan as damages for her medical expenses?

    (A) Only if Penny has paid the $5,000 bill at the time of trial.

    (B) Only if $5,000 is the reasonable value of the medically necessary services that Dr. Quinn provided.

    (C) Only if Dr. Quinn is a licensed physician.

    (D) Only if Penny's own health insurance will not cover the treatment.

27. Which of the following circumstances will preclude an injured plaintiff from recovering damages for lost or diminished earning capacity?

    (A) The plaintiff was an unemployed child at the time of injury.

    (B) The plaintiff returned to her pre-injury job before trial.

    (C) The plaintiff was an adult who was not employed outside of the home at the time of injury but instead was a full-time caregiver for his young children.

    (D) None of the above.

28. What are some of the factors that a jury will consider in determining damages for lost earning capacity?

ANSWER:

29. Peterman was severely injured in an automobile accident in which Davidson was at fault. As a result of his injuries, Peterman was unable to work for three months. Additionally, Peterman will require long-term nursing care to help him meet his daily living needs. In an action for negligence, Peterman will be entitled to recover several items of damages for personal injuries. Which of the following items of damages, if any, must be discounted to present value?

    (A) Damages for Peterman's pain and suffering.

(B)   Damages for wages lost before trial.

(C)   Damages for long-term daily nursing care.

(D)   Both (B) and (C).

30.   Patterson was injured in the course of his employment at Dockers Inc. As a result of his injuries, Patterson will not be able to return to his job at Dockers, nor will he be able to re-enter the workforce in any capacity. At the time of his injury, Patterson was earning $40,000 per year. At the time of trial, Patterson had a remaining worklife expectancy of 10 years. At trial, experts estimated that Patterson's salary would increase over the course of the remaining 10 years by 2% annually as a result of cost-of-living increases; 3% annually due to general increases in industry productivity; and 2% annually as a result of merit-based bonuses. In an action for personal injuries against Dockers Inc., what would be an appropriate method for discounting Patterson's damages for lost wages to present value?

(A)   Include increases due to industry productivity and merit-based bonuses in an estimation of Patterson's total lost wages and discount by a discount rate based on the current yield for a junk bond.

(B)   Include increases due to industry productivity and merit-based bonuses in an estimation of Patterson's total lost wages and discount by a discount rate based on the current yield for a triple-A rated corporate bond.

(C)   Include increases due to cost-of-living, industry productivity and merit-based bonuses in an estimation of Patterson's total lost wages and discount by a discount rate based on the current yield for a junk bond.

(D)   Include increases due to cost-of-living, industry productivity and merit-based bonuses in an estimation of Patterson's total lost wages and discount by a discount rate based on the current yield for a triple-A rated corporate bond.

31.   What are some of the types of harms for which a plaintiff can recover noneconomic damages in a personal injury case?

ANSWER:

32.   Patty slipped on an improperly maintained deck at a local pool and suffered a lacerated leg. Patty's Aunt Alice, a physician, treated Patty's injuries. Alice provided the medical services gratuitously. If Patty brings an action against the operator of the pool, what will be the measure of her recovery?

A.   Patty will be entitled to recover the reasonable value of the medical services that Alice provided.

(B)   Patty will be entitled to recover only the costs of any supplies Alice used to treat her.

(C)   Patty will be entitled to recover the reasonable value of the medical services that Alice provided only if the operator acted recklessly or intentionally.

(D)   Patty will not be entitled to recover any damages for medical expenses because she did not incur any medical expenses.

33.   Pierson injured her rotator cuff in an auto accident for which Davidson was at fault. As a result of her injuries, Pierson has lost some mobility in her arm and suffers from severe pain. All of the physicians who have examined Pierson have agreed that a corrective surgery would restore much of Pierson's mobility and alleviate her pain. However, Pierson has refused to have the corrective surgery. In an action for damages by Pierson against Davidson, which of the following will be true?

(A)   Pierson will be entitled to recover damages for her pain and suffering as a result of the rotator cuff injury because a defendant must take an injured plaintiff as she finds her.

(B)   Pierson will be entitled to recover damages for her pain and suffering if the surgery carries a real but slight risk of failure.

(C)   Pierson will be entitled to recover damages for her pain and suffering if she lacks the means to pay for the surgery.

(D)   Pierson will not be entitled to recover damages for pain and suffering under any circumstances.

34.   Harrison is injured in the course of his employment at Electric Company. As a result of his injuries, Harrison will be unable to return to work for several years. If Harrison and his wife, Wilma, bring an action for damages against Electric Company, which of the following is true?

(A)   Harrison will be entitled to recover damages for lost wages and pain and suffering, and Wilma will be entitled to recover damages for lost financial support and loss of companionship.

(B)   Harrison will be entitled to recover damages for lost wages and pain and suffering, and Wilma will be entitled to recover damages for loss of companionship.

(C)   Harrison will be entitled to recover damages for lost wages and pain and suffering, and Wilma will be entitled to recover damages for lost financial support.

(D)   Harrison will be entitled to recover damages for lost wages and pain and suffering, but Wilma will not be entitled to recover any damages.

35. Assure the same facts as in Question 34. Harrison and his wife, Wilma, brought an action for damages against Electric Company in a comparative fault jurisdiction. If a jury determines that Harrison was 30% at fault for his injuries, which of the following will be true?

   (A) Wilma will be barred from recovering damages for loss of consortium.

   (B) Wilma's recovery will be reduced in proportion to Harrison's fault.

   (C) Wilma will be entitled to recover 30% of her damages from Harrison and 70% of her damages from Electric Company.

   (D) Wilma's recovery will be unaffected by Harrison's fault.

36. Industrial cleaning chemicals were spilled on Poppins during the course of her employment. Poppins suffered minor chemical burns from the spill. She also has an increased risk of developing certain cancers as a result of her exposure to the chemicals. If Poppins brings an action for damages presently, which of the following is true?

   (A) Poppins can collect damages for the injuries from her burns and damages for her increased fear of developing cancer if she demonstrates to a reasonable certainty that she will develop cancer in the future.

   (B) Poppins can collect damages for the injuries from her burns and damages for any future medical expenses relating to cancer treatment if she demonstrates to a reasonable certainty that she will develop cancer in the future.

   (C) Poppins can collect damages for the injuries from her burns but must file a second action to recover damages for her medical expenses relating to cancer if and when she develops cancer.

   (D) Poppins cannot collect damages for injuries relating to future cancer treatment because such damages are too speculative.

37. Watson was severely injured in an auto accident for which Davis was at fault. Several months later, Watson died in an airplane crash. What potential claims against Davis exist?

   (A) Watson's Estate possesses a survival action against Davis.

   (B) Watson's Beneficiaries possess a wrongful death action against Davis.

   (C) Watson's Estate possesses a survival action against Davis, and Watson's Beneficiaries possess a wrongful death action against Davis.

   (D) No claims against Davis survive Watson's death.

38. Parker was severely injured in an auto accident for which Dickerson was at fault. Several months later, Parker died as a result of her injuries. If Parker's Representative

brings both a survival and a wrongful death action against Dickerson, which of the following will be true?

(A) Parker's Estate can recover damages for the wages Parker would have earned over the course of her natural lifespan.

(B) Parker's Estate can recover damages for the wages Parker would have earned over the course of her natural lifespan, and Parker's beneficiaries can recover damages for the loss of financial support from Parker.

(C) Parker's Estate can recover damages for the wages Parker lost between the accident and her death, and Parker's beneficiaries can recover damages for the loss of financial support from Parker.

(D) Parker's Estate cannot recover damages for lost wages, but Parker's beneficiaries can recover damages for the loss of financial support from Parker.

39. Dr. Doolittle failed to properly perform a tubal ligation on Paulette Patterson. As a result, Paulette and her husband conceived a child. Paulette ultimately gave birth to the baby. Which of the following best describes the Pattersons' likely recovery in an action against Dr. Doolittle?

(A) The Pattersons are likely to recover the damages for the pregnancy itself, including pain and suffering during the delivery and labor, as well as damages for the cost of rearing the baby because the Pattersons have a claim for wrongful pregnancy rather than wrongful birth.

(B) The Pattersons are likely to recover the damages for the pregnancy itself as well as damages for the cost of rearing the baby if the baby is born disabled.

(C) The Pattersons' recovery likely will be limited to damages for the pregnancy itself regardless of the health of the baby.

(D) The Pattersons will not be entitled to any recovery because they failed to mitigate their damages by placing the baby up for adoption.

40. Recently, the state of Calizona passed the following statute:

> In a tort action to recover damages for injury or loss to person or property, the amount of compensatory damages that represents damages for noneconomic loss shall not exceed the greater of $250,000 or an amount that is equal to three times the economic loss of the plaintiff in the tort action to a maximum of $350,000 for each plaintiff not to exceed a maximum of $500,000 for each occurrence that is the basis of that tort.

After the statute went into effect, Wendy was seriously injured while using a defective product at her home in Calizona. Wendy and her husband, Harold, filed an action against the manufacturer in Calizona state court. The jury awarded Wendy and Harold damages as follows:

Past and Future Medical Expenses	$500,000
Past and Future Lost Wages	$250,000
Pain and Suffering	$1 million
Loss of Consortium (loss of companionship only)	$500,000
	$2.25 million

If the manufacturer files a post-judgment motion for reduction of the verdict based on the new statute, how should the court rule?

(A) The court should grant the motion and remit the jury verdict to $1.25 million.

(B) The court should grant the motion and remit the jury verdict to $1.45 million.

(C) The court should grant the motion and remit the jury verdict to $1.6 million.

(D) The court should deny the motion because neither Wendy's nor Harold's damages for noneconomic losses are greater than three times Wendy's economic losses.

41. While failing to maintain a proper lookout, Bertie drove her car in reverse and collided with Hewlett's old jalopy. Hewlett was uninjured, but his jalopy suffered damage to the body of the car. Several mechanics estimated that it would cost $2800 to repair the jalopy. However, the mechanics also agreed that the body damage would not affect the drivability of the jalopy. Immediately before the accident, Hewlett's jalopy had a "bluebook" value of $560. After the accident, the jalopy had a bluebook value of $500. In an action by Hewlett against Bertie, what is the likely measure of Hewlett's recovery for the damage to the jalopy?

ANSWER:

42. While driving too fast for conditions, Door lost control of his car and collided with a car driven by Potter. Potter was uninjured, but Potter's car was destroyed. In an action by Potter against Door, which of the following is true?

(A) Potter will be entitled to recover both the pre-tort market value of the car and damages for the loss of use of the car during the length of time reasonably necessary to obtain a replacement car.

(B) Potter will be entitled to recover both the pre-tort market value of the car and damages for the loss of use of the car only if the car was used primarily for commercial purposes.

(C) Potter will not be entitled to recover both the pre-tort value of the car and damages for the loss of use of the car because the pre-tort value of the car already encompasses the right to use the car.

(D) Potter will not be entitled to recover both the pre-tort value of the car and damages for loss of use because Potter's recovery would exceed the pre-tort fair market value of the car.

43. Broker held 100 shares of stock in Company XYZ in an account for Client. On March 1, Broker sold the shares without Client's consent for the prevailing market price of $100 per share. On May 15, the market price rose to $120 per share. Client did not discover Broker's misconduct until Client ordered Broker to sell the shares on June 1. On June 1, the market price was $110 per share. The market price fell to $75 per share on July 1. Client eventually sued Broker for conversion of the shares. When the case

went to trial on Dec. 1, the market price had risen to $125 per share. Which best describes Client's likely measure of recovery?

(A) Client's recovery will be limited to $100 per share because it was the market price at the time of conversion.

(B) Client will be entitled to recover $120 per share because a reasonable investor could not have replaced the stock before May 15.

(C) Client will be entitled to recover $110 per share because a reasonable investor could have replaced the stock by July 1.

(D) Client will be entitled to recover $125 per share because Client has no obligation to replace the stock until Client recovers damages from Broker.

Questions 44–46 are based on the following hypothetical:

A fire caused by the tenants of a neighboring apartment destroyed Palmer's apartment. All of Palmer's furniture, clothing and personal belongings were destroyed in the fire. One of the items destroyed in the fire was an autographed photograph of Palmer with his favorite rock star. The picture was a snapshot taken by a friend of Palmer's on the night that Palmer's band performed as the opening act for the rock star.

44. In an action by Palmer against the other tenants for damages, which of the following best describes the likely measure of recovery for Palmer's destroyed clothing?

(A) Palmer is likely to recover the pre-fire market value of the clothing.

(B) Palmer is likely to recover the cost to replace the clothing with new clothing.

(C) Palmer is likely to recover the original purchase price of the clothing.

(D) None of the above.

45. In which of the following ways may Palmer prove the value of the destroyed clothing?

(A) Palmer may offer his opinion as to the value of the clothing as long as he explains the basis for his opinion.

(B) Palmer may offer his opinion as to the value of the clothing only if he corroborates that opinion with supporting documents such as the original receipts.

(C) Palmer may offer his opinion as to the value of the clothing only if Palmer has professional experience in buying or selling clothing.

(D) Palmer must offer independent expert testimony to establish the value of the clothing.

46. Which of the following factors will the jury likely be permitted to consider in determining an award of damages for the destroyed photograph?

i. The cost of developing the film.

ii. Palmer's sentimental feelings about the photograph.

iii. The cost of purchasing the film.

iv. The rate paid by newspapers and magazines for photographs of the rock star.

(A)   iv only.

(B)   i and iii.

(C)   i, iii and iv.

(D)   All of the above.

47.   Outdoor Advertising leased space in a building owned by LaSalle Realty. Outdoor Advertising installed a large advertising sign on the roof of the building in violation of the terms of the lease. When Outdoor Advertising removed the sign, portions of the roof were damaged. LaSalle Realty sued Outdoor Advertising to recover damages for the injury to the roof. At trial, experts estimated that the fair market value of the building immediately before Outdoor Advertising installed the sign was $2 million, and that after the sign was removed, the fair market value was $1.8 million. Experts also estimated that repairing the damage to the roof would cost $600,000. What are the best arguments for awarding LaSalle Realty the cost to repair the roof? What are the best arguments for limiting LaSalle Realty's recovery to the $200,000 diminution in value?

ANSWER:

48.   Under which of the following circumstances is the landowner most likely to recover the cost to repair the injury to the land?

(A)   The landowner seeks $5000 to repair a hole in a sand dune that served as a tide breaker when the property diminished in value by $10,000 as a result of the hole in the dune.

(B)   The landowner seeks $300,000 to re-build a home on her property when the pre-tort value of the home was $198,000 and the landowner used the home as her primary residence.

(C)   A non-profit organization seeks $800,000 to re-build an apartment building when the pre-tort value of the apartment building was $500,000 and the organization received a loan to purchase the building on the condition that the organization maintain it as low income rental housing.

(D)   All of the above.

Questions 49–50 are based on the following fact pattern:

Bunyan entered Loud's land and chopped down 50 of Loud's walnut trees. Bunyan then used his trusty ox, Babe, to haul the walnut trees off of Loud's land. In the course of removing the walnut trees, Babe trampled some small shrubs surrounding the orchard. Loud sued Bunyan to recover damages for the removal of the walnut trees and for the destruction of the shrubs.

49.   Which of the following best describes the likely measure of Loud's recovery for the lost walnut trees?

   (A)   Loud will be entitled to the market value of the walnut trees at the time of removal only if the walnut trees had reached commercial maturity at the time that Bunyan removed them.

   (B)   Loud will be entitled to the current market value of mature walnut trees discounted to present value if the trees had not yet reached commercial maturity when Bunyan removed them.

   (C)   Loud will be entitled to the cost to replace the walnut trees if they had not yet reached commercial maturity at the time that Bunyan removed them.

   (D)   Loud will be entitled to three times the market value of the walnut trees at the time of removal if Bunyan removed the trees in bad faith.

50.   Which of the following best describes Loud's likely recovery for the destruction of the shrubs?

   (A)   Loud will be entitled to recover the difference in the market value of the property with and without the shrubs.

   (B)   Loud will be entitled to recover the cost to replace the shrubs.

   (C)   Loud will be entitled to recover the original purchase price for the shrubs.

   (D)   Loud will not be entitled to recover damages because the shrubs have no marketable use.

51. Dirk drove his car over the curb and crashed the car into Peterson's house. In an action by Peterson against Dirk, which of the following facts would support an award of punitive damages?

(A) Dirk was driving with a suspended driver's license at the time of the accident.

(B) Dirk drove his car into Peterson's house as revenge because Peterson had beaten Dirk in a golf tournament.

(C) Both (A) and (B).

(D) Peterson will not be entitled to punitive damages because Peterson did not suffer any bodily injuries.

52. For what two purposes are punitive damages usually imposed?

ANSWER:

53. Palmer purchased a homeowner's insurance policy from Casualty Insurance Company. The policy purported to insure Palmer against any damage to or destruction of the home from fire. A faulty electrical outlet caused a fire in Palmer's home. Firefighters who were attempting to put out the fire sprayed water on Palmer's walls, causing damage to the walls and floor. Palmer filed a claim with Casualty. Casualty denied the claim on the ground that the damage was caused by water rather than fire even though controlling precedent clearly prohibited Casualty from denying the claim on this ground. In a lawsuit by Palmer against Casualty for breach of the insurance contract and bad faith denial of his claim, which of the following are true?

(A) Palmer may be entitled to punitive damages only if Palmer succeeds on the breach of contract claim.

(B) Palmer may be entitled to punitive damages only if Palmer succeeds on the bad faith claim.

(C) Palmer may be entitled to punitive damages if Palmer succeeds on either the breach of contract or bad faith claim.

(D) Palmer will not be entitled to punitive damages because both claims are essentially contract claims.

54. A Big-Mart employee stopped and searched Pullman on suspicion of shoplifting. The employee stopped Pullman because Pullman was African-American. The employee had no other basis to suspect Pullman of shoplifting, and Pullman had not, in fact, shoplifted. In an action by Pullman against Big-Mart, which of the following is true?

(A) Big-Mart may be liable for punitive damages only if Big-Mart's managers were aware that Big-Mart employees had a practice of stopping African-American customers but failed to end the practice.

(B) Big-Mart may be liable for punitive damages only if the Big-Mart employee who stopped Pullman exercised managerial responsibilities.

(C) Big-Mart may be liable for punitive damages if Big-Mart's managers were aware that Big-Mart employees had a practice of stopping African-American customers or the Big-Mart employee who stopped Pullman exercised managerial responsibilities.

(D) Big-Mart cannot be held vicariously liable for punitive damages based on the conduct of its employees.

55. Potter was seriously injured when the passenger-side airbag of the car in which she was riding failed to deploy during a high speed crash. Potter sued Neptune Motor Company, the company that manufactured the car, alleging that a defect in the airbag caused it to fail. Under which of the following circumstances might Neptune be liable for punitive damages in Potter's action?

(A) Neptune will be liable for punitive damages only if it intentionally designed the airbag to fail.

(B) Neptune will be liable for punitive damages if Neptune's internal testing data revealed that the airbag failed to deploy in one out of six crashes and Neptune decided to market the cars without correcting the defect.

(C) Neptune will be liable for punitive damages if Neptune's internal testing failed to detect the defect but more extensive testing would have revealed the defect.

(D) Neptune will be liable for punitive damages under all of the above circumstances.

56. Which of he following are appropriate factors for the jury to consider in determining an award of punitive damages?

(A) The financial condition or wealth of the defendant.

(B) The extent of harm to the plaintiff.

(C) The plaintiff's litigation costs.

(D) All of the above.

57. What "guideposts" did the Supreme Court identify in *BMW v. Gore* as indicators that an award of punitive damages is unconstitutionally excessive?

ANSWER:

58. Pittman sued Hospitality Inn alleging that Hospitality Inn knowingly let him a room that was infested with bedbugs. A jury found for Pittman, awarding him $5,000 in compensatory damages and $200,000 in punitive damages. Under which of the following circumstances would an appeals court most likely uphold the award of punitive damages if Hospitality Inn challenges the award as unconstitutionally excessive?

   (A) The award cannot be upheld under any circumstances because the ratio of punitive to compensatory damages exceeds 9-to-1.

   (B) Pittman suffered only minor injuries because he discovered the bed bugs shortly after settling into the room, but other guests had suffered from severe pain and serious medical complications as a result of their exposure to bedbugs.

   (C) Pittman suffered only minor physical injuries because bedbug bites generally do not pose serious medical risks. However, several other guests also suffered minor physical injuries from bedbug bites.

   (D) Hospitality Inn's managers had failed to report to its corporate headquarters a previous $100,000 punitive damages award imposed in a discrimination lawsuit.

59. Peters sued Officer alleging that Officer conducted an unconstitutional search of Peters' home in violation of 28 U.S.C. § 1983. The jury found that Officer had knowingly and intentionally acted unconstitutionally but that Peters suffered no compensable damage. If the jury also awards Peters $1 in nominal damages, will Peters be entitled to punitive damages?

ANSWER:

60. Under the law, a plaintiff is not automatically entitled to an injunction. Instead, the plaintiff must qualify for an injunction by showing irreparable injury. Irreparable injury means:

(A) That the plaintiff has suffered a legal injury.

(B) That the plaintiff has suffered an injury in fact.

(C) That the plaintiff has suffered an injury that cannot be remedied with damages.

(D) That the plaintiff has suffered an injury and prefers equitable relief.

61. The Aquas soccer team operated in the City of Atlantis for thirty years. The City of Atlantis owned the stadium, Municipal Stadium, where the Aquas played and leased it to the team. Two years ago, the City entered into a ten-year lease with the soccer team to play in the stadium. However, Pete Poseidon, the owner of the Aquas, became discontented with soccer in Atlantis and announced that he would relocate the team to Treasure Island. He was disillusioned with the falling ticket sales in Atlantis, the lack of a modern stadium with luxury boxes, and the disrespect he felt the City exhibited toward him in not responding to his requests for a new stadium. In contrast, Treasure Island had agreed to build Poseidon a new stadium complete with luxury boxes and seat license fees for season tickets that would generate substantial income for the team. The State of Oceana in which Treasure Island is located also agreed to use lottery proceeds to fund the new stadium on Treasure Island. Most cities eagerly desire a professional sports team because of its positive impact on city pride and reputation, as well as the perceived economic benefits to the city.

The City of Atlantis decided it would not let the Aquas leave without a fight. The City sued the Aquas for breach of the lease agreement and sought specific performance of the lease requiring the Aquas to abide by the contract and play its home soccer games in Municipal Stadium for the remaining term of the lease. Does the City qualify for the requested injunction?

(A) Yes, because the claim is one for breach of contract.

(B) Yes, because the City can establish the requisite uniqueness.

(C) No, because of the difficult burden on the court.

(D) No, because of the public policy in favor of efficient breaches of contract.

62.   Assume the same facts in Question 61. What is the team's best argument against the issuance of the injunction?

ANSWER:

63.   Perfumania builds a new, state-of-the-art manufacturing plant near the outskirts of Old Town. The plant owners make a $30 million capital investment in the factory and employ over 300 people. The plant's residential neighbors are irritated by the flowery perfume smells that constantly emanate from the plant. The neighbors complain that they are unable to open their windows, enjoy the summer breeze, or use their decks due to the sickeningly sweet smell. The neighbors are quite upset by the annoying, but harmless smell, and seek an injunction to close down the plant. Will the neighbors prevail?

      (A)   No, because of the undue burden on Perfumania.

      (B)   No, because of the burden on the court.

      (C)   Yes, because of the balance of hardships in plaintiffs' favor.

      (D)   Yes, because of the intangible emotional distress.

64.   The Nimbes read in their local newspaper of a plan to build an apartment complex on their block. They learn that the opposite side of the street is zoned for multiple family dwellings. The Nimbes are concerned that the apartment will change the nature of their quiet residential neighborhood by increasing traffic, bringing in undesirable tenants, and diminishing their home value. Can the Nimbes seek an injunction to prevent the building of the apartment complex?

      (A)   Yes, because of the need to prevent legal harm in advance.

      (B)   No, because of the lack of a threat of harm.

      (C)   Yes, because of the irreversibility of building the complex.

      (D)   No, because the zoning code permits the land use.

65.   Molly Woo is a famous softball player for the Akron Aces. Her personality and fame attract great numbers of fans to the games. Woo enters into a contract with the Aces to play for three seasons. However, after a disappointing first year, Woo decides to sign with the Tampa Tempo due to the Tempo's excellence in developing players. The Aces sue Woo to enforce the contract and keep her in Akron. What result?

      (A)   Injunction granted because of Woo's unique status.

      (B)   Injunction denied because of the policy against personal servitude.

(C) Injunction denied because of the undue hardship to Woo.

(D) Injunction granted because of the policy of enforcing written promises.

66. Betty Lou wrote a song that her boyfriend, Sid Rockstar, later turned into a commercial success with his band, Vicious. When the two break up, Betty sues Sid for copyright infringement since he stole the lyrics and music to her song. Should Betty seek damages or an injunction as her remedy?

ANSWER:

67. Mrs. Kravitz is shocked to learn that her neighbor two doors down keeps a tiger for a pet in his back yard. She is fearful that the tiger will escape and harm her small children, Sally, Dick and Jane, and scare the other children in the neighborhood. Will the court issue an injunction requiring the neighbor to get rid of the tiger?

(A) No, because the tiger is the neighbor's property.

(B) No, because the tiger has not caused any harm.

(C) Yes, because a tiger is an inherently dangerous object.

(D) Yes, because the tiger poses a real threat of imminent harm.

68. A federal court holds that Online Inc. has illegally infringed a patent held by Engineering Inc. Engineering seeks an injunction against Online's continued use of the patent which will force Online to shut down part of its internet business. The district court grants the injunction, reasoning that Engineering incurred damages from the lost profits and that there is a strong public policy against patent infringement embodied in the U.S. Constitution. The court also reasons that Engineering's failure to request a preliminary injunction is irrelevant to its request for a permanent injunction. What is the flaw in the court's reasoning in support of the injunction?

(A) That the irreparable injury rule is satisfied.

(B) That the preliminary injunction is irrelevant.

(C) That public policy is relevant to granting injunctions.

(D) That injunctions are available in patent cases.

69. Macrocorp was found liable for monopolization in violation of the antitrust laws. The court found that Macrocorp engaged in illegal anticompetitive behavior through a series of contracts with its software licensees. If the court wants to issue a preventive injunction, which of the following provisions is appropriate?

    (A) Macrocorp must develop a new standard contract for software licensees.

    (B) Macrocorp must stop monopolizing the market through its software agreements.

    (C) Macrocorp must split into two separate companies, Macro and Micro.

    (D) Macrocorp must rewrite the existing contracts with its software licensees.

70. A prophylactic injunction:

    (A) is designed to stop the existing harm.

    (B) is designed to address the facilitators of harm with additional precautions.

    (C) is designed to correct the continuing consequences of past harm.

    (D) is not a valid type of injunction.

71. Animal rights protest groups are arrested and prosecuted for trespassing on private research lab property and for assaulting the lab employees. After finding that the protestors violated the federal PET (Protection of the Endangered against Testing) statute, the court orders the protestors to "stop blocking or interfering with public access to lab property and physically abusing persons at the lab." When protestors fail to comply with the first injunction, the court orders the protestors to stay 35 feet away from the lab grounds. What types of injunctive measures has the court issued against the protestors?

    (A) Reparative and preventive.

    (B) Structural and reparative.

    (C) Preventive and prophylactic.

    (D) Prophylactic and structural.

72. Susie Smith is an administrative assistant for a high-powered lawyer, Bob Grant, at a large law firm in Cleveland. Ever since she began work for Mr. Grant six weeks ago, she has been subjected to his constant harassment, including sexist jokes, physical

touching, and requests for dates. When she complained to the office manager, the manager told her to stop being so sensitive and to get a sense of humor. Embarrassed, Smith did not file a written complaint with the manager, even though she knew two other employees had previously complained about Grant. Smith did, however, sue the law firm for violations of federal employment laws. Assume that the law firm has lost on the issue of liability, and the court is now proceeding to determine the appropriate remedy in the case. As the attorney for Ms. Smith, what type of injunctive provisions would you propose to the court?

ANSWER:

73. CHICK, the California Higher Institute of Curricular Knowledge, is an all-female teachers' college run by the state of California. CHICK claims that its pedagogy of discussion and consensus building is uniquely suited to women, and that such a learning environment would be destroyed by a coed student population. The California Court of Appeals finds that CHICK's exclusion of male students violates the Equal Protection Clause. What is the appropriate measure of injunctive relief?

(A)   Order California to build a similar college for men.

(B)   Order California to close CHICK.

(C)   Order California to privatize CHICK and divest public funds.

(D)   Order California to allow men access to CHICK.

74. Structural injunctions are often claimed to be illegitimate forms of injunctive relief. What are the arguments against the validity of structural injunctions?

ANSWER:

75. A class of prisoners brings suit claiming that their right of access to the courts was denied by the prison's failure to provide an adequate law library. The evidence at trial proves that one inmate was prevented from seeking access to the court due to his illiteracy. The trial court enters an injunction mandating extended law library hours, adequate lighting, legal materials for Spanish-speaking inmates, paralegals, an adequate number of typewriters, and noise decibel restrictions. What result on appeal?

(A)   The injunction is upheld because the scope of relief matches the scope of the harm.

(B)   The injunction is upheld as necessary to prevent future harm.

(C) The injunction is overturned because the scope of the injunction is overbroad.

(D) The injunction is overturned because it provides for services not constitutionally required.

76. Cola Co. enters into a contract with Spice-o-Life for monthly installments of flavorings needed to manufacture its soda pop. After six months, Spice fails to deliver the contractual amount of flavoring. Apparently, Spice has found a more lucrative customer in Energy 2000, who is willing to pay Spice twice as much as Cola. Cola is unable to find any other company who can provide the flavorings for its soda because Spice is the only company with the distinctive combination of flavorings Cola needs. Cola sues Spice for breach of contract. What result?

(A) Spice does not have to perform the contract, but must pay for Cola's extra costs.

(B) Spice does not have to perform the contract, but must pay for Cola's future lost profits.

(C) Spice must perform the contract and pay for Cola's future lost profits.

(D) Spice must perform the contract.

77. Fred Father was ordered to pay $325 per month in child support for his 12-year-old daughter until the age of 18. The amount of support was calculated based on Father's income. Five years later, Father is laid off from his job and is earning no income. Which of the following is true?

(A) Father can seek modification of the support order based on changed factual circumstances.

(B) Father can seek termination of the support order based on changed factual circumstances.

(C) Father can seek modification of the support order based on his good faith compliance with a substantial part of the order.

(D) Father can seek termination of the support order based on his good faith compliance with a substantial part of the order.

78. Rocky Husband is arrested on domestic violence charges. He is sentenced to jail until completion of a court-approved counseling program, Batterers' Treatment Program. Rocky objects to the counseling program, which is run by a religious organization. If Rocky challenges the counseling program as a violation of the First Amendment, what remedies are available to Rocky?

(A)   An injunction.

(B)   An injunction, mandamus, and contempt.

(C)   An injunction, mandamus, and declaratory relief.

(D)   An injunction, contempt, and declaratory relief.

79. Shoe Co. is concerned that its competitor, Footworks, is replicating one of its shoe styles in a cheaper model in violation of the trademark laws. The shoes are scheduled to appear on the shelves in Footworks stores in four days. Assuming that Shoe Co. files a complaint with a viable claim regarding the violation of its intellectual property, which of the following injunctions could it seek?

(A) Temporary injunction.

(B) Temporary and preliminary injunctions.

(C) Temporary, preliminary and permanent injunctions.

(D) Preliminary and permanent injunctions.

80. Most domestic violence laws provide for an expedited process through which *ex parte* restraining orders are issued against alleged batterers. What are the constitutional arguments for and against these types of orders?

ANSWER:

81. The state of Utopia has enacted legislative measures to provide for school vouchers allowing students in public districts to transfer to private schools with the use of voucher credit. A recent Utopia Supreme Court opinion upheld the constitutionality of the small pilot program for this voucher system. However, a ten-year-old U.S. Supreme Court opinion struck down a similar voucher system in the state of Franklin. In July, Utopia school administrators begin full implementation of the voucher system. A plaintiff class comprised of teachers, students, and parents sues the State of Utopia claiming that the voucher program is unconstitutional and requests a preliminary injunction. What is the likely result of their request?

(A) Denied because of the balance of hardships in the state's favor.

(B) Denied because it does not further the public interest.

(C) Granted because of the likelihood of success on the merits.

(D) Granted because of the irreparable injury to the plaintiffs.

82. LeBaron Fly, a superstar high school basketball player, was suspended from the team hours before the beginning of championship play. The school superintendent heard a media account claiming that Fly had accepted gifts and money from an athletic booster in violation of the amateur player rules. The Superintendent immediately suspended Fly from the team. Fly sues the Superintendent for violation of his due process rights in federal district court, and seeks a temporary injunction allowing him to play in the championship. Will the temporary injunction be granted?

(A) Yes, if the Superintendent receives actual notice.

(B) Yes, if there are efforts to notify the Superintendent.

(C) No, because of the lack of an imminent threat of harm.

(D) No, because there is no denial of due process.

83. Princess Sabrina, a famous international figure, has been continually hounded by the media and paparazzi since her marriage to a Prince. One reporter in particular, Sam Sleaze, has harassed her and continually invaded her privacy over the last ten years. In the past six months, Sleaze has printed thirty stories about Sabrina and her children. While no article or picture has appeared in the last few weeks, Sabrina is interested in taking legal action to stop Sleaze from violating her privacy, and files a lawsuit against him. What type of injunctive relief is a court likely to award Sabrina at this stage of the litigation?

(A) Temporary relief.

(B) Temporary and preliminary relief.

(C) Preliminary relief.

(D) Preliminary and permanent relief.

84. The City of Acadia has been swamped with protestors from a Save the Whales campaign. A tidal wave of protestors has caused damage to the town buildings and property and blocked traffic for miles. Yesterday, the protestors got out of hand and assaulted some of the local fishermen during a particularly violent protest. The Acadian police would like to obtain a temporary restraining order to stop the protest scheduled for today. The police file a complaint with the court, and make no attempts to contact the protestors prior to the *ex parte* hearing. Will the court issue the requested temporary injunction?

(A) No, because there is no immediate harm threatened.

(B) No, because there were no efforts to notify the defendants.

(C)   Yes, because actual notice to the defendant is not required.

(D)   Yes, because *ex parte* injunctions are authorized by the court.

85.   What are the four legal requirements for the issuance of a preliminary injunction?

ANSWER:

86.   Temporary, preliminary, and permanent injunctions differ in:

(A)   Duration.

(B)   Eligibility criteria.

(C)   Time of imposition.

(D)   All of the above.

87.   Charlie's Chips sells snacks on a street corner at First and Main in the middle of a university campus. Charlie has sold snacks at this location for four years, but is finding that business has dwindled this year due to the construction of a new university library on the other side of campus. Charlie moves his snack cart to a new location at Second and Elm right in front of the library and business picks up. The university, however, receives a complaint from Coffee Grinders etc., who is licensed by the university to sell coffee at the library. The university files a complaint against Charlie for trespass and seeks a preliminary injunction enjoining him from selling coffee anywhere on campus. What is a court likely to do?

(A)   Enjoin Charlie from selling snacks anywhere on campus.

(B)   Permit Charlie to sell snacks at the library location to preserve the status quo.

(C)   Permit Charlie to sell snacks at First and Main to preserve the status quo.

(D)   Deny the preliminary injunction which fails to advance the public interest.

88.   Discuss the requirements of Federal Rule of Civil Procedure 65 C which provides that "[n]o restraining order or preliminary injunction shall issue except upon the giving of security by the applicant, in such sums as the court deems proper. . . ."

ANSWER:

89. Which of the following constitutes a proper circumstance for the imposition of contempt?

(A) A mother accidentally pays $10,000 too little in child support.

(B) A corporate defendant refuses to produce a document that it has, but does not want the plaintiff to know of the document.

(C) A company fails to adopt workplace policies that would avoid future violations of the law similar to those committed in the past.

(D) A defendant refuses to conduct himself appropriately in the courtroom after the court orders him to behave.

90. The government brings a contempt motion against Microcorp seeking to enforce a consent decree that prohibited Microcorp from entering licensing agreements that tied products to its operational software in violation of the antitrust laws. The court found that the challenged conduct did not violate the terms of the consent decree which were vague on this point. The court should:

(A) Deny the motion because contempt cannot be used to enforce consent decrees.

(B) Hold the government in contempt for bringing a frivolous motion.

(C) Deny the motion because Microcorp is not in violation of the order.

(D) Deny the motion and issue a revised order clarifying the vague terms.

91. Susan McDonagal refused to testify as a witness in the infamous Bluewater trial against President Clintex. The court ordered McDonagal jailed until she agreed to testify. Susan ultimately served two years for her refusal to testify, at which time the Bluewater case had ended. What kind of contempt remedy did the Court impose?

(A) Summary contempt.

(B) Criminal contempt.

(C) Civil coercive contempt.

(D) Civil compensatory contempt.

92. Why are procedural safeguards required prior to the imposition of the contempt remedy?

ANSWER:

93. In a divorce action, Husband is ordered to pay spousal support to Wife. Husband does not pay the ordered support. The domestic relations court conducts a hearing and takes evidence, finding that Husband has the ability to pay. The court orders Husband to pay the $4000 amount of support owed in thirty days or face up to six months in jail. What result on appeal?

    (A) No contempt against Husband due to the lack of willful violation.

    (B) No contempt against Husband because the court failed to conduct the necessary procedures prior to imposing criminal contempt.

    (C) Contempt upheld against Husband because the court properly measured the amount of the civil compensatory fine.

    (D) Contempt upheld against Husband because the court properly crafted the civil coercive remedy so that the defendant could purge the contempt remedy.

94. What are the legal strategies and defenses defendants can use to defend against motions for contempt?

ANSWER:

95. During a trial in an unfair competition case, the judge repeatedly instructs defendant, a taxicab driver, to be silent and to stop disrupting the proceedings. The judge warns defendant's counsel to control his client, and the lawyer replies: "I am doing the best I can with him, your Honor." After an adverse ruling, the defendant stands up and begins to storm out of the courtroom, muttering expletives as he goes. The judge:

    (A) May order the defendant to be taken immediately into custody.

    (B) May order the defendant to be taken into custody after a proper hearing.

    (C) May order the defendant to be taken into custody after a proper hearing and an opportunity for the defendant to be heard.

    (D) May not order the defendant into custody, and must refer the case to the criminal prosecutors' office for further review.

96. The Geographic Association of Lady Softballers (GALS) refused to play ball for its parent corporation, Major League, when the company used discriminatory tactics in promoting the new softball league. The GALS reacted strongly to the company's sexist policies and began to picket the fields, assault league employees and patrons entering the field, and destroyed softball league property. The League brought a tort action against the GALS, and the court ordered them to stop all trespasses, assaults, and

destruction of property. GALS failed to follow the court's order, and sixty days later, the court conducted a hearing under which it required proof of violations of the order to be proven beyond a reasonable doubt. It ordered GALS to pay $60,000 for past violations of the injunction, and announced that future violations of the order would be assessed a fine of $10,000 per assault. The court's order constitutes:

(A) Valid criminal contempt because the court required proof beyond a reasonable doubt.

(B) Invalid criminal contempt because the court did not utilize the required criminal procedural safeguards.

(C) Valid civil coercive contempt because the court announced future fines that could be avoided by the defendants.

(D) Invalid civil coercive contempt because the court failed to conduct the required hearing.

97. If the court instead assessed fines against GALS measured by the amount of property damage, pain and suffering, and other loss caused by its violations of the order, it would constitute:

(A) Valid civil coercive contempt.

(B) Valid civil compensatory contempt.

(C) Valid criminal contempt.

(D) Compensatory damages.

98. Joe agreed to pay Builder $1 million to construct a new Bananas restaurant for him. Joe is a new franchise owner of the national Bananas chain that is known for its banana-shaped restaurants and delicious banana splits. Builder negligently constructs the restaurant by making it the shape of a hot dog, rather than a banana. Joe estimates it will cost $250,000 to make the necessary alterations to the building. Can Joe sue Builder for restitution?

    (A) No, because Builder has no unjust benefit to disgorge.

    (B) No, because Joe has suffered irreparable injury.

    (C) Yes, because Joe is entitled to punish Builder for the breach of contract.

    (D) Yes, because Joe is entitled to be compensated for his losses.

99. Tenant leased Landlord's building to manufacture its specialty toys. Tenant produces brain challenger puzzles for toddlers made out of wood. Tenant discovered a shrink wrap machine hidden in one of the closets of the building and began to use it to package its toys. The machine saved Tenant the $20/day cost of paying workers to wrap the toys by hand. One day, while visiting the plant, Landlord discovered that Tenant was using the machine. Landlord had not used the machine in over ten years, and offered to rent it to Tenant for $100 per month. Tenant refused the offer, and Landlord sued Tenant for restitution. What is the legal theory upon which restitution can be based?

    (A) Quantum meruit.

    (B) Constructive trust.

    (C) Quasi-contract.

    (D) Rescission.

100. Assume the same facts as in Question 99. What is the most appropriate measure of restitution in this case?

    (A) The rental value of the machine.

    (B) The market value of the machine.

    (C) The cost savings from the use of the machine.

    (D) The total profits from the sale of the toys.

101. The University solicits bids for artists to design the mural at its new student activity center. Artista submits a low bid of $5000 to design the plans for the mural. Artista's bid is accepted contingent upon funding from the National Arts Council. She shows her initial designs to the University board and it approves her work. However, six months into the project, the University's funding for the mural is lost. Artista has completed 90% of the design work when she is told that the project is cancelled pursuant to the terms of the contract. By this time, she has expended $9000 worth of work on the project. What action can Artista take against the University?

    (A) Sue in quasi-contract for $5000.

    (B) Sue in quasi-contract for $9000.

    (C) Sue in quantum meruit for $5000.

    (D) Sue in quantum meruit for $9000.

102. Lego Builders wanted to compete for a bid to build the new city hall in town. It then began receiving sub-contract bids. The lowest bid was made by Bionicle Builders for $180,000, which was $25,000 less than the next lowest bid. Based upon this low bid, Lego submitted its general bid to the City Council. Lego's general bid was $20,000 lower than the City Council originally anticipated, due to the low sub-bid from Bionicle. The City Council accepted Lego's bid. After the acceptance, Bionicle informed Lego that there had been a mistake in computing the sub-bid, and that the correct amount was $220,000. Lego was unaware of this mistake. In a suit for rescission of the contract with Lego, Bionicle should:

    (A) Not succeed because the mistake was made before the bid was accepted.

    (B) Not succeed unless Lego actually knew or should have known of the mistake.

    (C) Succeed because the mistake was bilateral.

    (D) Succeed because this was a unilateral mistake.

103. Accountant volunteers to help his elderly neighbor with her taxes. Unbeknownst to him, the neighbor has a confusing array of stocks and properties that makes the taxes quite complicated. Accountant ends up spending five times as long on the taxes as he expected, and loses a significant amount of time at the office from working on his neighbor's account. When the ungrateful neighbor refuses to even say thank you for the tax preparation, Accountant decides to sue in restitution. What result?

    (A) Accountant will receive restitution in the amount of the services rendered.

    (B) Accountant will receive restitution in the amount of the time lost at work.

(C)   Accountant will be denied restitution because he was a volunteer.

(D)   Accountant will be denied restitution because neighbor had no unjust benefit.

104.   Distributor, a food service company, enters into oral negotiations with Almondia, a locally owned company that manufacturers gourmet foods for a trendy almond diet. Distributor wants to establish an exclusive arrangement for distributing the Almondia products in the southern states. During the initial negotiations, the parties agreed on the important terms of the agreement, but had not yet worked out all the details. Both parties were excited about the new deal, and Almondia assured Distributor, "Don't worry. We'll work the rest of the things out." Assuming that he had the deal sealed, Distributor hired additional workers, leased larger space, and purchased delivery equipment. Shortly thereafter, Almondia told Distributor that it had signed a deal with Florida Brothers to handle the distribution. Which of the following theories would help Distributor prevail in a lawsuit against Almondia?

(A)   Implied-in-fact contract.

(B)   Promissory estoppel.

(C)   Unjust enrichment.

(D)   Quasi-contract.

105.   Pizza driver is involved in a three-car accident while racing to deliver pizzas on time. Driver suffers injuries to his leg and requires medical treatment. The medical expenses are paid by his insurance company. After investigation, it is established that Driver and the driver of a second car were both causes of the accident. Driver was speeding in order to follow his restaurant's new policy of promising customers a 29-minute delivery. The restaurant also promised their drivers that they would cover them for any legal problems regarding the policy. What restitution claims are likely to be raised in this case?

ANSWER:

106.   Insurance Co. insured the chief executive officer of Big Corporation for $3 million. The CEO, a young man of 45, represented in his insurance application that he was in good health, had no preexisting medical conditions, and was a non-smoker. Less than one year after issuance of the policy, CEO died of a heart attack. Upon investigation, Insurance Co. discovered that CEO had in fact been a heavy smoker. What result if Insurance Co. sues for restitution?

(A)   Rescission of the contract and retention of the $3 million.

(B)   Enforcement of the contract and payment to Big Corporation of $3 million.

(C)   Enforcement of the contract and payment to Insurance Co. of the additional cost of premiums for smokers.

(D)   Rescission of the contract, retention of the $3 million, and return of the premiums paid.

107.   Public Agency sues Computer Co. for failure to deliver 100 computer screens which it says it purchased for $200 each. Agency still wants the screens, and seeks their immediate delivery. At trial, there is no evidence proven of a written contract or any testimony about an offer and acceptance. The two parties who negotiated the alleged contract for each side no longer work for the organizations and cannot be located. Evidence is presented that Public Agency wrote a check to Computer Co. for $20,000 and that Computer Co. deposited that check in its bank account. Upon what basis would Public Agency be entitled to relief?

(A)   Rescission.

(B)   Express contract.

(C)   Quasi-contract.

(D)   Implied-in-fact contract.

108. Which of the following is not an equitable restitution remedy?

    (A) Quasi-contract.

    (B) Constructive trust.

    (C) Equitable lien.

    (D) Accounting of profits.

109. In recent cases before the U.S. Supreme Court, the Court has distinguished equitable from legal restitution. What are the hallmark characteristics of equitable restitution?

ANSWER:

110. Winifred and Harry are newlyweds. Harry's parents own farm land and agree to let Harry and Winifred build a home on the land worth $20,000. The couple uses $30,000 of their savings to secure a $140,000 mortgage for the house. Harry helps the contractor build the house in order to save money. Winifred helps paint the house and does small jobs on the construction, services valued at approximately $22,000. Ten years later, Winifred and Harry divorce, splitting everything equally. At the time of the divorce, the house and land are valued at $220,000 and the mortgage has been paid in full by Winifred and Harry. If Winifred successfully sues Harry's parents under a theory of constructive trust, what amount will the court award?

    (A) $22,000.

    (B) $85,000.

    (C) $100,000.

    (D) $107,000.

111. Assume the same facts as in Question 110, except that Winifred sues under a theory of equitable lien. What amount will the court award?

    (A) $22,000.

    (B) $85,000.

(C) $100,000.

(D) $107,000.

112. Bonnie Ray is the latest TV cooking sensation. Her new cookbook, "The Hot Mama's Guide to Baking" is number one on the bestsellers list. It turns out, however, that Bonnie stole all of the recipes from her mother-in-law. She had told her mother-in-law that she wanted to have all the family's secret recipes to continue the traditions in her own family. However, Bonnie really intended to publish the recipes in her new book. What equitable theory of restitution would assist Mother-in-law in disgorging all of Bonnie's unjust profits?

(A) Equitable lien.

(B) Quasi-contract.

(C) Constructive trust.

(D) Accounting of profits.

113. Bob and Gretta decide to move in together. Bob moves into Gretta's house that she owns and which is valued at $80,000. The couple decides to add a second floor to the house, and Bob contributes $55,000 of his own money from a savings account to pay for the cost of the construction work. Five years later, the remodeled house is valued at $150,000. However, after 6 years, the couple has grown apart and Bob moves out. When Gretta refuses to compensate Bob for his contribution to the house, he brings a lawsuit against her. What restitution remedy is available to Bob?

(A) Quantum meruit for the value of his services.

(B) Constructive trust for the appreciated value of the house.

(C) Equitable lien for the debt owed to Bob.

(D) Indemnification by Gretta for the cost of the construction work.

114. In modern times, civil justice advocates have petitioned the legal process to try and obtain redress for the injustice of slavery in the United States. The slavery reparations cases seek, among other things, monetary relief on behalf of the survivors of slaves for their forced labor. Restitution has been the primary legal avenue upon which these reparations claims have been based. How would you frame these arguments for slavery reparations as restitution claims?

ANSWER:

115. Erb's Root Beer infringes on the trademark of Beerman's Brew. Erb's takes the design and color of Beerman's label as its own. Beerman's proves that this caused consumers to believe that Erb's product was affiliated with the popular best-selling Beerman's beer. At trial, the evidence shows that during the time of the infringement, Erb's earned $3 million in sales. No evidence is submitted as to whether or not Beerman in fact lost any sales from the infringement. Erb's documents show that it cost them $2 million to produce the root beer, and that Erb's engaged in a targeted advertising campaign during the time of infringement that generated $250,000 in new sales. What amount is Beerman likely to recover as a measure of restitution?

(A) $3 million.

(B) $1 million.

(C) $750,000.

(D) $0.

116. LeMar Ivory was the treasurer of the Great Lakes church when he embezzled $200,000 from church funds. He gave $100,000 of the monies to his girlfriend, Betty. She purchased a Mercedes Benz automobile for $50,000 and purchased stocks with the remaining $50,000. The stocks have now increased in value to $100,000 and the car has depreciated in value to $30,000. Ivory fled to Costa Rica and cannot be located. The church sues Betty for restitution of the stolen funds. What result?

(A) The church is awarded $100,000.

(B) The church is awarded $130,000.

(C) The church is awarded $150,000.

(D) The church is awarded $200,000.

117. Sally, Dick and Jane are neighbors on the Gulf Coast of Florida. During a particularly bad hurricane, Sally and Dick move into Jane's two-bedroom house to ride out the storm. The homes of Sally and Dick are destroyed in the storm, and Jane offers to let the neighbors stay. Sally and Dick begin to pay Jane a reasonable monthly rent. After three years, the roommates decide to build a third bedroom and second bathroom onto the house. Dick builds the addition himself and uses $10,000 of his savings to purchase construction supplies. This increases the value of Jane's home to $200,000, from the original price of $60,000, though part of this increase is due to market factors related to the lack of housing after the storm's destruction. One year later, Jane notifies her roommates that she is going to be married, and needs them to move out of the house. When Dick asks for compensation for his addition to the home, Jane refuses. If Dick sues Jane for restitution, what result?

(A) Dick will be awarded an equitable lien for the value of his services.

(B) Dick will be awarded an equitable lien in the amount of his savings and services.

(C) Dick will be awarded a constructive trust for the return of his savings.

(D) Dick will be awarded a constructive trust for the value of the appreciated house.

118. Laurel and Hardy have been passing out anti-war leaflets against the government's military action in a shopping center in Village. The police warn them twice that they must stop leafleting or they will be arrested and prosecuted for criminal trespass. Laurel quits passing out the pamphlets. Hardy continues and is arrested and prosecuted by the Village. Laurel sues for declaratory relief, stating that the criminal trespass statute as applied violates his First Amendment rights. Is Laurel entitled to declaratory relief?

(A) No, because he has stopped passing out the pamphlets.

(B) Yes, because he wants the court to order the police to stop arresting protesters.

(C) No, because there is no definite and concrete controversy between Laurel and Village.

(D) Yes, because the controversy is ripe.

119. Howell works as a regional vice-president for the XYZ Chemical Corporation, which specializes in direct sales of heavy duty cleaning supplies to large industrial plants. XYZ employed Howell pursuant to a written contract which contained a provision prohibiting "competition with the business of the company in any respect for a period of five years following dismissal or termination of employment." Howell is wondering whether he could quit the company and start a business that specializes in Internet sales of cleaning supplies. XYZ has not yet entered the market for Internet sales. Howell files an action seeking a declaration as to what the meaning of "competition" is under the employment contract. Is he entitled to declaratory relief?

(A) No, because the controversy is hypothetical and not adverse.

(B) No, because declaratory judgments are not available in contract.

(C) Yes, because the controversy is ripe.

(D) Yes, because there is an actual controversy.

120. The San Diego Ships, a professional basketball team in the American Basketball Association (ABA) wants to relocate to Los Angeles. The ABA, afraid of antitrust liability under a recent ruling prohibiting it from blocking team relocations, reluctantly schedules the Ships' home games in Los Angeles. The League simultaneously files an action seeking a declaratory judgment stating that the antitrust laws permit it to fine teams for moving in violation of the League's policies agreed to by the membership teams. Is the ABA entitled to declaratory relief?

    (A)   No, because the move is completed.

    (B)   No, because the controversy is not definite and concrete.

    (C)   Yes, because the controversy is ripe.

    (D)   Yes, because the controversy relates to an important legal issue.

121.   Why would a litigant choose a declaratory judgment remedy over other remedies?

ANSWER:

122.   Natalie Merchant brings an action against the Ten Thousand Maniacs band seeking a declaration that she, and not the Maniacs, owns the copyrights to a series of songs she wrote as a member of the band. A California court determines that Merchant is the proper copyright holder, and issues declaratory relief in her favor. Eight months later, Merchant discovers that the Maniacs are still selling and licensing her songs as if they in fact owned the copyrights. How can Merchant enforce her declaratory judgment?

    (A)   She cannot enforce the DJ which is simply an authoritative and definitive statement of the legal relations of the parties.

    (B)   She can enforce the DJ by filing a new complaint seeking restitution of the profits made by the Maniacs.

    (C)   She can enforce the DJ by seeking contempt for the Maniacs' intentional failure to comply with the decision regarding the copyrights.

    (D)   She can enforce the DJ by seeking further relief in the amount of the Maniacs' profits.

123.   McGwire is a sailor on a merchant marine vessel, The Cardinal. While on shore leave in Japan, he gets into a dispute with Soza over who is the greatest baseball hitter of all time. The dispute erupts into physical violence, and Soza suffers serious bodily injuries. MLB Steamship Company, the owner of The Cardinal and McGwire's employer, files suit seeking a declaration that if Soza sues, MLB is not vicariously liable for Soza's injuries. Is MLB entitled to declaratory relief?

    (A)   No, because it does not terminate the uncertainty.

    (B)   No, because it relates to a completed event.

    (C)   Yes, because the controversy is ripe.

    (D)   Yes, because the controversy is adverse.

124. Identify the components of the Uniform Declaratory Judgments Act that guide the issuance of declaratory relief in state court.

ANSWER:

125. A middle school teacher is arrested for sexually molesting one of his students. He is arraigned on charges of sexual molestation, assault, and a lesser misdemeanor. The teacher's insurance company sues for declaratory judgment seeking an order stating that there is no coverage for molestation. How should the court rule?

    (A) Issue a declaratory judgment because there is an actual controversy.

    (B) Issue a declaratory judgment because the case is ripe.

    (C) Deny the declaratory judgment because the order will not terminate the uncertainty.

    (D) Deny the declaratory judgment because the defendant seeks a tactical advantage.

126. John and Paul enter into a contract for the sale of John's plumbing business. John's lawyer prepares the terms of the deal providing that Paul will assume ownership of the business upon payment of $45,000. Paul is not represented by counsel nor does he consult a lawyer. In small type on the back of the contract, the lawyer inserts a paragraph that gives John the unilateral right to cancel the contract within 6 months if he believes that Paul is not handling the business appropriately. Five months later, John sues Paul seeking rescission of the contract and return of the business to his ownership. Which of the following defenses might be available to Paul?

(A) *In pari delicto.*

(B) Unconscionability.

(C) Unclean hands.

(D) Estoppel.

127. What is the difference between the remedial defenses of *in pari delicto* and unclean hands?

ANSWER:

128. Landlord leases a commercial property to a private childcare center. To comply with child safety laws, the center builds a chain-link fence around the playground. Landlord drives by the property and notices the fence does not comply with the zoning code, subjecting him to penalties. Landlord talks with the center's director and says he understands the center's need for the fence. Based on this conversation, the center takes no action to change the fence. Four weeks later, landlord sends the center an eviction notice because of the non-conforming fence which violates the terms of the lease. What remedial defense would best assist the center?

(A) Estoppel.

(B) Laches.

(C) Unclean hands.

(D) Unconscionability.

129. Neighbor brings a lawsuit against Homeowner seeking damages for trespass to his land. Homeowner installed a new swimming pool in her backyard that extends 4 feet onto

Neighbor's property. Homeowner says that she is surprised at the lawsuit given the fact that Neighbor's roof extends 2 feet onto her property. What remedial defense might be available to Homeowner?

(A)   *In pari delicto.*

(B)   Waiver.

(C)   Unclean hands.

(D)   Unconscionability.

130.   On May 10, 2003, plaintiff files a lawsuit against Doctor alleging malpractice related to a treatment performed on June 1, 2000. The applicable statue of limitations in the state is three years. After filing and serving the complaint, plaintiff's attorneys wait four years before beginning discovery due to their work overload associated with a fourteen-month class action trial. By then, Doctor has retired, the office has closed, and patient files more than three years old have been destroyed by the staff. Which of the following remedial defenses could Doctor assert to bar plaintiff's recovery?

(A)   Statute of limitations.

(B)   Unclean hands.

(C)   Waiver.

(D)   Laches.

131. Why does the law permit plaintiff's conduct to serve as a bar to recovery?

ANSWER:

132.   Plaintiffs, passengers in a car, sue the driver of a truck who negligently caused a car accident. They seek recovery for their physical and emotional injuries in the accident. Defendant wants to argue that the plaintiffs' own misconduct of drinking bars their recovery. What result?

(A)   No available defense because plaintiffs are bringing an action at law.

(B)   No available defense because the facts do not support any remedial defense.

(C)   No recovery for plaintiffs because of the merger of law and equity.

(D)   No recovery for plaintiffs because of their comparative fault.

133. The legal maxim that "equity does not reward those who sleep on their rights" describes what equitable remedial defense?

    (A) Laches.

    (B) Statute of Limitations.

    (C) Unclean hands.

    (D) *In pari delicto*.

134. Baker and Simpson entered into a contract for the sale of 500 widgets. Simpson refused to deliver the widgets to Baker at the agreed upon date because Simpson had found a buyer who would pay a higher price for the widgets. In a breach of contract action by Baker against Simpson, which of the following is true?

   (A) Baker will be entitled to recover attorney fees from Simpson if Simpson breached the contract without legal excuse or justification.

   (B) Baker will be entitled to recover attorney fees from Simpson if Simpson willfully breached the contract.

   (C) Baker will not be entitled to recover attorney fees from Simpson if Simpson's breach was an "efficient breach."

   (D) Baker will not be entitled to recover attorney fees from Simpson regardless of Simpson's reasons for breaching the contract.

135. Polly Pilot sued Able Airlines on behalf of herself and all similarly situated pilots. In her suit, Pilot alleged that Able breached its collective bargaining agreement with its pilots by failing to reimburse pilots for certain professional licensing fees incurred by the pilots. Able agreed to pay the class an amount equal to the value of all the licensing fees paid by its pilots. If Pilot files a motion to recover attorney fees, which of the following is true?

   (A) The court can order Able to pay Pilot's attorney fees because Pilot is a prevailing party in the litigation.

   (B) The court can order Pilot's attorney fees paid out of the settlement fund because each of the class members benefited from the fund.

   (C) The court cannot order Pilot's attorney fees paid out of the fund unless all class members attempt to collect a share of the fund.

   (D) The court cannot order Pilot's attorney fees paid out of the fund because Pilot benefited from the fund.

136. Pauline Plaintiff, a female applicant to the Metropolis Police Department, was rejected after she failed to achieve the necessary score on a physical aptitude test. Plaintiff sued the Metropolis Police Department alleging that the physical aptitude test had an impermissibly discriminatory impact on women in violation of Title VII of the federal Civil Rights Act. Metropolis defended the claim on the ground that the test measured

physical abilities that were bona fide occupational qualifications ("BFOQ"). Plaintiff ultimately prevailed on the merits of her claim. If Plaintiff seeks attorney fees, which of the following will be true?

(A) Plaintiff will be entitled to recover her attorney fees because she is a prevailing party.

(B) Plaintiff will not be entitled to recover attorney fees because Metropolis did not act with discriminatory intent.

(C) Plaintiff will not be entitled to recover attorney fees unless Metropolis lacked a good faith basis for claiming that the test measured BFOQs.

(D) Plaintiff will not be entitled to recover attorney fees if she recovered compensatory damages or backpay.

Questions 137–139 are based on the following fact pattern.

Patterson, who is confined to a wheelchair, attempted to view a popular movie at Dressel's Multi-Plex 15 Theaters but was denied access because the theater in which the movie was playing was not wheelchair accessible. Patterson sued Dressel, alleging that Dressel violated the federal Americans with Disabilities Act (ADA) by failing to make reasonable accommodations for people in wheelchairs. Patterson sought statutory damages and an order requiring Dressel to make all 15 of its theaters accessible. While the litigation was pending, Patterson and Dressel entered into a settlement agreement. Under the terms of the agreement, Dressel agreed to submit to entry of a consent decree ordering it to make one of its theaters wheelchair accessible and to rotate all first-run movies through that theater. In exchange, Patterson agreed to forgo all claims for damages and all claims pertaining to the remaining 14 theaters. The court then entered the consent decree, incorporating the terms of the settlement agreement.

137. If Patterson files a motion to recover attorney fees from Dressel, which of the following will be true?

(A) Patterson will not be entitled to recover attorney fees because Patterson's claim was not resolved by a trial on the merits of Patterson's claim.

(B) Patterson will not be entitled to recover attorney fees because Patterson did not recover damages and instead recovered only equitable relief.

(C) Patterson will not be entitled to recover attorney fees because Dressel only has to make one movie theater wheelchair accessible.

(D) Patterson will be entitled to recover attorney fees because the court incorporated the terms of the settlement agreement into the consent decree and the decree requires Dressel to make one theater wheelchair accessible.

138. Assuming Patterson is entitled to recover attorney fees, which of the following will be true?

    (A) Patterson will be entitled to recover the full amount of the fee billed by Patterson's attorney because Patterson achieved more than a technical victory.

    (B) Patterson will be entitled to recover an amount reduced to reflect Patterson's limited success.

    (C) Patterson will be entitled to recover for only those hours which Patterson's lawyer expended on pursuing claims pertaining to the one theater which will be modified.

    (D) Patterson will be entitled to recover only nominal attorney fees because Patterson did not prevail on all of his claims.

139. Assuming Patterson is entitled to recover attorney fees, what other factors, if any, might the court consider in determining the reasonableness of the fee award?

ANSWER:

140. Parker sued Sheriff pursuant to 28 U.S.C. § 1983, alleging that Sheriff unlawfully detained Parker without probable cause in violation of Parker's constitutional rights. More than 10 days before trial, Sheriff served Parker with a written offer to accept judgment for $50,000 inclusive of costs and attorney fees. At the time of the offer, Parker had incurred $10,000 in attorney fees. Parker rejected the offer, and the case went to trial. At trial, a jury returned a verdict for Parker in the amount of $30,000. The court entered judgment on the verdict, and Parker filed a motion for attorney fees, seeking $25,000 in fees. Which of the following best describes how the court should rule on the motion?

    (A) The court should award Parker $25,000 in attorney fees plus costs because Sheriff's offer of judgment improperly offered one lump sum for both the substantive claim and costs and attorney fees.

    (B) The court should award Parker $25,000 in attorney fees because the $30,000 judgment for Parker recovered at trial combined with Parker's $25,000 in attorney fees exceed Sheriff's $50,000 offer of judgment.

    (C) The court should award Parker $10,000 for Parker's pre-offer attorney fees but refuse to award any post-offer attorney fees.

    (D) The court should deny Parker's motion because Parker's recovery at trial was less favorable than the offer of judgment.

PRACTICE FINAL EXAM: QUESTIONS

Instructions: **This exam consists of 44 questions, some of which are multiple choice questions and some of which are short answer questions. Try to answer these questions in no more than 90 minutes.**

141. Bradford entered into a contract to purchase Sally's used car for $1500. The bluebook value of the car was $2000. After Bradford and Sally entered into the contract, Tina offered to purchase Sally's car for $1800. Sally refused to deliver her car to Bradford. In an action for breach of contract by Bradford, what will be the measure of damages if Bradford does not cover?

    (A) $500

    (B) $1500

    (C) $2000

    (D)   Bradford is not entitled to damages.

142. Your client is considering whether to file suit for an injunction or declaratory judgment. How would you advise your client as to the advantages of declaratory relief?

ANSWER:

143. Plaintiff suffered damage to her cornea as a result of an infection caused by a defective contact lens. Plaintiff was treated by a physician and put on a medicine regimen that lasted ten days to cure the infection. Plaintiff also had to undergo a surgical procedure to repair the damage to her cornea. Plaintiff missed two months of work while recovering from the surgery. Medical experts agree that most people who contract this type of infection make a full recovery and have no lasting vision problems. However, a small number of people suffer recurring vision problems as a result of the corrective surgery. Plaintiff's vision has been completely restored and, thus far, she has shown no signs of recurring vision problems. In an action by Plaintiff against the manufacturer of the contact lens, which of the following will not be recoverable?

(A)   The reasonable value of the surgery because Plaintiff acted unreasonably in having a surgery that posed a risk of future complications.

(B)   The medical expenses related to the treatment of any vision problems Plaintiff might suffer in the future because such expenses are too speculative.

(C)   Lost wages for the time that Plaintiff missed work because Plaintiff's employer continued to pay her salary during that period.

(D)   Plaintiff will be entitled to recover all of the above.

144.   Larry Litigator is up against Sammy Slime in yet another personal injury case. Given Slime's general reputation for dishonesty, Larry is concerned that Slime will refuse to play by the court's rules and will fail to provide the appropriate documents during discovery. At the initial conference in the case, Larry asks for a general order against Slime requiring him to produce all relevant documents in the case. What result?

(A)   Injunction granted due to Slime's propensity towards dishonesty.

(B)   Injunction granted because the order conforms to the regular discovery rule.

(C)   Injunction denied because there is no irreparable injury.

(D)   Injunction denied because there is no threat of imminent harm.

145.   Baker and Simpson entered into a contract for the sale of land. Simpson refused to deliver title to the land. If Baker sues Simpson for breach of contract, which of the following are true?

(A)   Baker will be entitled to a jury trial only if Baker seeks money damages.

(B)   Baker will be entitled to a jury trial only if Baker seeks specific performance of the contract.

(C)   Baker will be entitled to a jury trial if Baker seeks either money damages or specific performance.

(D)   Baker will not be entitled to a jury trial

146.   Betty Crocker Hershey, the owner of Sweets-R-Us, has soured on the candy business. She decides to turn her business over to her son, Mr. Clean. Betty agrees to employ Mr. Clean as corporate president, and they enter into a written contract for twenty years at an annual salary of $350,000. Mr. Clean loves being president and is thankful for the once-in-a-lifetime opportunity to run a family business. However, after three years of retirement, Betty is tired of eating bon-bons all day. She fires her son and resumes the

presidency of Sweets-R-Us. Mr. Clean sues to enforce the terms of the contract. What result?

(A)   Specific performance is granted because of Clean's detrimental reliance.

(B)   Specific performance is granted because of the uniqueness of the contract.

(C)   Specific performance is denied because Clean can find another job.

(D)   Specific performance is denied because it is difficult to enforce.

147.   A class of women prisoners in the state of Gilead bring suit alleging violations of the Eighth Amendment's prohibition of cruel and unusual punishment for their conditions of confinement. The inside of the prison is unsanitary and kept at a temperature of 50 degrees. Women who are pregnant are denied adequate medical care. It is also established at trial that guards routinely sexually harass and assault the women. As the attorney for the successful plaintiffs, what injunctive relief will you request from the court?

ANSWER:

148.   Porter was seriously injured when an industrial press that Porter was operating malfunctioned. Porter sued the manufacturer of the press for personal injuries. Porter sought damages for pain and suffering as well as for medical expenses and diminished earning capacity. At trial, Porter's counsel made the following closing argument to the jury:

> Let's talk about one element of damages. We have talked about pain and suffering. What would be fair compensation for pain and suffering? Ladies and gentlemen of the jury, it is entirely up to you. But let me make a suggestion. If you think about what it is like for Porter to go through one day with the pain that Porter has, what do you think would be fair? Would it be $100 to go through that in a day? Would it be $75? I want to be scrupulously fair in my request to you. So I am going to suggest that you award Porter $50 a day for the pain and suffering. Now consider that there are 365 days in a year and 30 years of pain and suffering that Porter should be compensated for. So that's $547,500 for 30 years of pain and suffering.

What objections, if any, might defense counsel raise to this closing argument?

ANSWER:

149. Homeowner bought a house for $250,000 from a man anxious to sell, and secured the purchase with a $240,000 mortgage. After moving into the house, Homeowner noticed seepage from the sewage disposal and called in a repair person to fix the problem. It was discovered after further investigation that the land was not an approved home site because of the lack of sufficient topsoil. Homeowner now wants to cancel the contract and be paid for the costs of moving and hiring an expert to assess the problem. What restitution remedy can Homeowner seek?

(A) Implied-in-fact contract.

(B) Quasi-contract.

(C) Quantum meruit.

(D) Rescission.

150. Approximately 300 minority Big City police officers claim that a test administered to determine promotions to sergeant is racially biased. They seek a preliminary injunction to prohibit the City from making sergeant promotions pending the outcome of their lawsuit. The district court finds that under the law, it is a close question as to whether the officers have a meritorious claim. It also finds that any temporary denial of a promotion could later be addressed by monetary damages. Based on these findings, how should the court rule on the request for preliminary injunction?

(A) Grant the injunction because of the likelihood of success on the merits.

(B) Grant the injunction because of the harm to the plaintiffs.

(C) Deny the injunction because of the undue hardship to the City.

(D) Deny the injunction because of the lack of irreparable injury.

151. The court held a hearing in an admiralty case as to why contempt sanctions should not issue for an attorney's failure to appear at trial. The case had been continued three times to accommodate the attorney's schedule. The attorney told two federal judges that he was appearing before the other on the same date, when in fact he was appearing before neither. What action can the judge take?

(A) Jail the attorney for 10 days.

(B) Order the attorney to pay $2500.

(C) Order the attorney to pay the costs of the defendants' attorney fees.

(D) Order Rule 11 sanctions for frivolous conduct.

152. Which of the following cases would *not* support an award of punitive damages?

(A) A jubilant casino patron hugs his dealer after winning a large sum of money, causing serious physical injury to the dealer.

(B) A frustrated law student punches her professor after receiving a disappointing grade, causing serious physical injury to the professor.

(C) A repair person knowingly misrepresents the length of time needed to complete the repairs in negotiating a service contract with a customer.

(D) An award of punitive damages would be appropriate in all of the above.

153. Father wants Daughter to move back home to Small Town from the dangers and high prices of New York City. He promises to give his successful daughter her own interior design business. Father lets Daughter use a piece of business property he owns, and Daughter secures a loan in the amount of $25,000 to purchase office equipment and inventory for her business. Daughter runs a successful business and voluntarily gives her Father a 10% share of the business profits. Ten years later, Father informs Daughter that he is selling the property in order to obtain funds to retire to Florida. Daughter is incensed and sues her Father in restitution for his promise to give her the business. What result?

(A) Constructive trust to Daughter for the value of the property.

(B) Equitable lien to Daughter in the amount of the improvements to the property.

(C) Constructive trust denied because of absence of fraud or breach of trust.

(D) Equitable lien denied because of the lack of property to secure.

Questions 154–155 are based on the following fact pattern:

Victor suffered a severe head injury during a bar fight with Dan. Victor never regained consciousness after suffering the head injury. He spent several weeks in a coma, and ultimately died as a result of the head injury.

154. In an action by Victor's Representative against Dan, which of the following most accurately describes the Estate's recovery?

(A) Victor's Estate will be entitled to recover damages for the medical expenses Victor incurred before death, pain and suffering, and the wages Victor would have earned over the course of his natural worklife span.

(B) Victor's Estate will be entitled to recover damages for the medical expenses Victor incurred before death and Victor's pain and suffering.

(C) Victor's Estate will be entitled to recover damages for the medical expenses Victor incurred before death and the wages Victor would have earned over the course of his natural worklife span.

(D)   Victor's Estate will be entitled to recover damages for the medical expenses Victor incurred before death.

155.   In a wrongful death action against Dan brought on behalf of Victor's next of kin, which of the following most accurately describes the probable recovery?

(A)   Victor's Beneficiaries will be entitled to recover damages for the loss of Victor's financial support and for the loss of his companionship.

(B)   Victor's Beneficiaries will be entitled to recover damages for the loss of Victor's financial support only.

(C)   Victor's Beneficiaries will be entitled to recover damages for the loss of Victor's companionship only.

(D)   Victor's Beneficiaries will not have a wrongful death claim against Dan.

156.   Sampson agreed to sell 15 used delivery trucks to Bivens at a price of $7500 per truck. The fair market value of the trucks was $7000 per truck. Bivens refused to accept delivery of the trucks. Sampson resold the trucks to Thompson at a private sale for $3000 per truck. In an action for breach of contract by Sampson, what will be the measure of Sampson's damages?

(A) $7500 per truck.

(B) $4500 per truck.

(C) $500 per truck.

(D)   Sampson is not entitled to damages.

157.   The People Against Coffee are planning a protest next week against Coffee Incorporated at its national headquarters. The police would like to avoid any harm to people and property from the protest, and thus seek a temporary injunction to prohibit the protest. The police file a complaint and motion for temporary relief, and deliver a copy of the papers to the protest leader. The court conducts an *ex parte* hearing. Will the temporary injunction be granted?

(A)   No, because there was inadequate notice to the defendant.

(B)   No, because there is no legal harm threatened.

(C)   No, because the threatened harm is not imminent.

(D)   No, because *ex parte* hearings are unconstitutional.

158.   Paula Smith sued President Clintex for alleged sexual harassment. The court issued an order carefully defining "sexual relations" for purposes of questioning in the case. During deposition, President Clintex testified that he did not have sexual relations with

Mona Monica. Subsequently, on national television, Clintex admitted that he had "inappropriate relations" with Monica. Upon the plaintiffs' motion for contempt, the judge awards the plaintiff $90,000 for its attorney fees in bringing the contempt motion and the costs of the deposition in which Clintex lied, and says she will conduct a hearing if Clintex so requests. What result on appeal?

(A) The criminal contempt remedy is invalidated for improper procedures.

(B) The civil compensatory remedy is upheld as valid.

(C) The civil compensatory remedy is invalidated for improper procedures.

(D) The criminal contempt remedy is upheld as valid.

159. While driving too fast for conditions, Davis lost control of the car that Davis was driving and collided with Patterson. Patterson was uninjured, but Patterson's car suffered substantial damage. In an action by Patterson against Davis for damage to the car, what is the likely measure of Patterson's recovery?

(A) Patterson is entitled to recover the cost to repair the car as long as the car can be restored to its pre-accident condition.

(B) Patterson is entitled to recover the cost to repair the car if the car can be restored to its pre-accident condition and the cost to repair the car does not exceed the pre-accident value of the car.

(C) Patterson is entitled to recover the cost to repair the car if the car can be restored to its pre-accident condition and Patterson has a personal reason for repairing the car.

(D) Patterson is not entitled to recover the cost to repair the car under any circumstances.

160. A test preparation company, Get U Ready, has been accused of sending representatives to take secure standardized tests in order to obtain confidential questions. Secure questions are kept secret by the creators of the tests and reserved for possible use on future tests. A lawsuit is filed against Get U Ready and trial is set for a date eight months later. In the interim, the testing company would like to obtain a court order barring Get U Ready from using copies of its test questions. What relief is available to the standardized testing company at this stage of the litigation?

(A) Temporary injunction.

(B) Preliminary injunction.

(C) Temporary, preliminary, and permanent injunctions.

(D) Temporary and preliminary injunctions.

161. Beasley Middle School ordered 200 t-shirts at a cost of $4.00 per t-shirt from Super Tees. The t-shirts contained a specially designed logo commemorating graduation which incorporated the class year and the date of graduation. Super Tees purchased 200 blank t-shirts at a cost of $1.00 per shirt. Super Tees also purchased ink for the shirts at a cost of $0.30 per shirt. Super Tees estimated its overhead expenses to be $0.20 per shirt. After Super Tees completed 100 t-shirts, Beasley repudiated the contract. Super Tees sold the remaining 100 blank t-shirts for $0.50 per shirt and paid $0.10 per shirt to ship the 100 blank shirts to the purchaser. In an action for breach of contract, what will be the measure of Super Tees damages?

    (A) $800

    (B) $760

    (C) $650

    (D) $500

162. Davidson, a restaurant server, intentionally spilled hot coffee on Peters, a customer, after Peters failed to leave Davidson an adequate tip. Peters suffered serious burns. Peters sued Davidson for personal injuries. If Peters' personal injury action is tried to a jury, which of the following is true?

    (A) A jury must impose punitive damages on Davidson if it concludes that Davidson acted intentionally.

    (B) A jury may impose punitive damages on Davidson if it concludes that Davidson acted intentionally.

    (C) Only the judge can impose punitive damages on Davidson even if the jury finds that Davidson acted intentionally.

    (D) Punitive damages are not appropriate in this case.

163. Billy agrees to sell his baseball card collection to Bobby for $150. Billy knows that there are no valuable cards in his collection, but he tells Bobby that there are two cards worth over one hundred dollars each. Bobby's roommate, who works at a baseball trading card store, overhears the conversation and interrupts to tell Bobby that there are no valuable cards in the collection. Bobby still goes through with the purchase. When he later discovers that the card collection is worth only $20, he sues for breach of contract. What defenses are available to Billy in the action?

    (A) Waiver.

    (B) Estoppel.

(C) Estoppel and Waiver.

(D) Unconscionability.

164. In a bench trial for personal injury damages, Plaintiff offered expert testimony to establish her future lost wages. Plaintiff's expert included an upward adjustment in Plaintiff's future wages to account for future increases in wages due to increases in the cost of living. Judge Grumpy, the presiding judge, excluded this testimony, prohibiting Plaintiff from offering any estimates of future wage increases based on increases in the cost of living. Judge Grumpy ruled that such evidence was too speculative. In awarding Plaintiff damages for future lost wages, Judge Grumpy discounted Plaintiff's damages to present value based on a the current market yield for certain bonds issued by the federal government. What basis, if any, does Plaintiff have to challenge Judge Grumpy's award of damages for future lost wages?

ANSWER:

165. Big, Bad and Boom fireworks opens up a new manufacturing site in Tylersville, where it employs 10 workers. The fireworks factory spews toxic chemicals into the air that have a putrid odor. Mrs. Small, who lives 3 blocks from the factory, develops lung problems. Upset and worried that she is seriously ill, Mrs. Small consults her doctor who believes the serious medical problem is caused by the fireworks plant. Can Mrs. Small seek an injunction to stop the hazardous pollution?

(A) No, because of the economic waste to Big, Bad and Boom.

(B) Yes, because of the serious physical and emotional harm to Mrs. Small.

(C) No, because of the public policy in favor of commercial manufacturing.

(D) Yes, because of Mrs. Small's preference for injunctive relief.

166. STOIL Co. brings suit seeking a declaratory judgment that a state excise tax levied on it for the storage of gasoline is invalid under the Commerce Clause and the Fourteenth Amendment of the Federal Constitution. The court should:

(A) Deny the declaratory judgment because there is no case or controversy.

(B) Grant the declaration because there is an actual controversy.

(C) Deny the declaratory relief because the claimant seeks an advisory opinion.

(D) Grant the declaration because it presents a hypothetical question.

167.   Big Films Industry makes a movie using a story it received in the mail from an eighteen-year-old novice writer from Indiana. Without contacting the writer, Big Films proceeds to make the movie. It gets the biggest star in Hollywood, Betty Devine, to play the lead in the film. Devine alone can generate $30 million in movie profits. The film is a box office smash and generates $65 million in revenues for the low-budget film that cost only $5 million to make. Writer sues Big Films for copyright infringement. If she is successful, what is the likely amount of recovery in restitution?

   (A) $10,000, the typical cost of a royalty payment to a new author.

   (B) $65 million, the total profits to Big Film.

   (C) $60 million, the total profits offset by costs to produce the film.

   (D) $30 million, the total profits offset by production costs and profits from Devine.

Questions 168–169 are based on the following fact pattern:

Farmer Brown owns a small farm. The property has been used by the Brown family as a farm for over 100 years. The property is divided into four fields. Shortly after planting one of the fields, Farmer Brown discovered that chemicals from a nearby manufacturing plant were leaching into the soil on that field. Experts agree that while the chemicals themselves are not harmful to humans, the chemicals have stripped the soil of vital nutrients, rendering the soil unfit for agriculture. Experts also agree that the chemicals can be removed from the soil, but that the soil cannot be restored to productive agricultural use. Farmer Brown brought suit against the owner of the manufacturing plant.

168.   What is the likely measure of recovery for damage to the land?

   (A)   Farmer Brown will be entitled to recover the cost to remove the chemicals from the soil unless the cost exceeds the pre-contamination value of the land.

   (B)   Farmer Brown will be entitled to recover the cost to remove the chemicals from the soil unless the cost exceeds the diminution in the value of the land.

   (C)   Farmer Brown will be entitled to recover the pre-contamination value of the land because the land is destroyed.

   (D)   Farmer Brown will be entitled to recover the diminution in value to the land because the damage to the land is permanent.

169.   What is the likely measure of recovery for the lost crops?

   (A)   Farmer Brown will be able to recover the lost profits that Brown would have earned on the crops.

   (B)   Farmer Brown will be entitled to recover the fair market value of the crops.

(C) Farmer Brown will not be entitled to recover damages for the lost crops because they will be duplicative of damages for the injury to the land.

(D) Farmer Brown will not be entitled to recover damages for the lost crops because they are too speculative.

170. The Urban City Transit Workers Union went on strike in reaction to the City's failure to provide adequate funding for the Union's health insurance costs. The district court found that the strike by public safety workers violated the federal labor laws and ordered the workers to return to work. When the workers had not returned to work five days later, the judge gave notice to the Union and conducted a hearing to address the workers' past violations of her order. The judge then ordered the Union to pay $10,000 per day until its workers returned to work. This fine is:

(A) Valid civil coercive contempt.

(B) Invalid civil coercive contempt.

(C) Valid criminal contempt.

(D) Invalid criminal contempt.

171. Plimpton worked for Big Brother Credit Card Company. Plimpton also held a Big Brother credit card for personal use. After Plimpton called in sick for several days in a row, Plimpton's supervisor at Big Brother accessed Plimpton's personal credit card records without authorization. Plimpton's supervisor was attempting to determine whether Plimpton was abusing her sick leave. When Plimpton discovered the unauthorized intrusion, Plimpton sued Big Brother for invasion of privacy. The evidence at trial revealed that several other employees had complained to Big Brother management that the same supervisor had accessed their personal credit card records. A jury awarded Plimpton $100,000 in compensatory damages for emotional distress and $1 million in punitive damages. If Big Brother challenges the award as unconstitutionally excessive, what arguments can be advanced to set aside the award? What arguments can be advanced to sustain the award?

ANSWER:

172. Explain the difference between the remedial defenses of laches and statute of limitations.

ANSWER:

Questions 173–174 are based on the following facts:

Software Co. entered into a three-year contract with Fashion Mavens (FM) to develop software for FM's use in delivering fashion consultations over the Internet. FM initially paid Software $60,000 to secure the contract, and agreed to pay Software royalties from future profits. One year into the contract, FM stopped paying royalties to Software in violation of the terms of the contract. After adversarial negotiations produced no agreement, Software sued FM to rescind the contract and seek payment of all profits FM generated from the use of its software products.

173.   What is the legal basis for Software's claim for rescission?

   (A)   The inadequacy of damages.

   (B)   The mistaken payment of royalties.

   (C)   The substantial breach of contract.

   (D)   The implied-at-law contract.

174.   Assume that the court grants Software's request for rescission. What is the proper measure of relief?

   (A)   The amount of profits made by FM using the software.

   (B)   The amount of profits made by FM attributable to the software and not attributed to FM's own contributions.

   (C)   The amount of profits made by FM attributable to the software and not attributed to FM's own contributions, offset by a return to FM of the $60,000.

   (D)   The amount of Software's loss under the contract.

175.   Iggy Insured entered into a contract for professional liability insurance with Massive Mutual. A client sued Insured for malpractice, and Insured tendered the claim to Massive Mutual for defense in accordance with the terms of the insurance contract. Massive Mutual refused to defend the claim. As a result, Insured had to retain an attorney at his own expense to defend against the client's claim. Insured ultimately prevailed in client's suit and sued Massive Mutual for breach of insurance contract and bad faith refusal to defend the claim. If Insured prevails on his breach of contract claim against Massive Mutual *only*, which of the following best describes what Insured's recovery will be?

   (A)   Insured will be entitled to recover the attorney fees he incurred in defending client's claims and the attorney fees he incurred in prosecuting his breach of contract claim against Massive Mutual.

   (B)   Insured will be entitled to recover the attorney fees he incurred in defending client's claims.

(C)   Insured will be entitled to recover the attorney fees he incurred in prosecuting his claims against Massive Mutual.

(D)   Insured will not be entitled to recover any of his attorney fees.

176.   Landlord rents an old racquetball building to New Church for a term of six years with an option to buy. New Church renovates the building to make it suitable for services. It adds many improvements to the building, adding a sanctuary, improving the grounds, and installing a kitchen. After six years, New Church is not able to purchase the building due to a lack of funds. Landlord is quickly able to rent the church building to another developing church group at double the monthly rent he was receiving from New Church. New Church requests that the Landlord reimburse it for the improvements it made to the building, but Landlord refuses, saying it was a risk the church took as a tenant. If New Church sues Landlord on an equitable restitution theory, what is the likely result?

(A)   Constructive trust awarded to New Church for the appreciation of the building.

(B)   Accounting of profits awarded to New Church in the amount of the increased rent.

(C)   Quantum meruit for the value of the church's construction services.

(D)   Equitable lien in the amount of the church's services and financial investments.

177.   Parker retained Anderson as counsel to represent Parker in a personal injury action. The retainer agreement between Parker and Anderson provided that Parker would pay Anderson 33% of any judgment or settlement that Parker ultimately obtained. Parker discharged Anderson and retained a new attorney, Baker. Baker ultimately settled Parker's claim for $500,000. Anderson sued Parker to recover attorney fees. What amount, if any, should Anderson be entitled to recover?

ANSWER:

178.   Contractor is denied a building permit by the town of Hudson. The administrative regulations provide that Contractor may appeal the denial within twenty days of the order. Sixty-two days later, Contractor files an action for declaratory judgment against the town. The declaration is inappropriate because:

(A)   The declaration will not terminate the uncertainty.

(B)   The controversy is not ripe.

(C)   The controversy is not definite and concrete.

(D)   The declaration is used for tactical advantage.

179. The Big Fig sued Newton Co. for trademark infringement because Newton Co. was selling a product with the same name as its product called "California Fig Syrup." The testimony at trial revealed that neither company's syrup is made from figs. How should the case be resolved?

    (A) Case dismissed because of plaintiff's unclean hands.

    (B) Judgment for Big Fig because of defendant's fraud.

    (C) Judgment for Big Fig because of defendant's unclean hands.

    (D) Case dismissed because of *in pari delicto*.

180. Dudley Do-Right sued the National Regulatory Commission ("NRC"), the State of Utopia and KMG Corp., seeking an injunction preventing the NRC and Utopia from granting KMG a permit to mine uranium. Do-Right contended that certain federal environmental laws prevented the NRC and Utopia from granting a permit until the permit applicant filed an environmental impact statement and that KMG had failed to file an environmental impact statement. Do-Right ultimately prevailed in his lawsuit, and the court issued an order enjoining the NRC and Utopia from granting the permit. If Do-Right files a motion to recover attorney fees, which of the following is true?

    (A) Do-Right will be entitled to recover his attorney fees because his lawsuit involves an important public policy issue.

    (B) Do-Right will be entitled to recover his attorney fees because his lawsuit will affect how the NRC and Utopia handle future permit applications.

    (C) Do-Right will not be entitled to recover his attorney fees because KMG will be able to obtain a permit once it files the environmental impact statement.

    (D) Do-Right will not be entitled to recover attorney fees because his lawsuit did not generate a determinative fund to which an identifiable class of third parties has a claim.

181. Specialty Products, Inc. agreed to manufacture a specially designed press for Manufacturer's assembly line. At the time of contracting, Manufacturer explained to Specialty Products that Manufacturer was in the business of manufacturing and selling widgets. Manufacturer explained that it needed the press to complete the manufacture of its widgets. Specialty Products delivered a press that did not fit into Manufacturer's assembly line. Manufacturer promptly sought repair of the press. In a breach of contract action by Manufacturer, what will be the measure of Manufacturer's damages?

    (A) Manufacturer will be entitled to recover the difference between the value of the press as delivered and value of the press as contracted for.

(B) Manufacturer will be entitled to recover its lost profits on the sale of widgets that it was unable to manufacture and sell while the press was being repaired.

(C) Manufacturer will be entitled to recover both the difference between the value of the press as delivered and value of the press as contracted for and Manufacturer's lost profits.

(D) Manufacturer will not be entitled to recover damages.

182. Surfer Dude enters into a contract with Best-O-Wax for 100 cans of surf board wax at a price of $5.00 per can. Best-O-Wax fails to deliver the wax due to a manufacturing error that leaves it with no inventory to sell. Dude is able to find 50 cans of OK-Wax for sale at $6.00 per can, but prefers the Best-O-Wax. Surfer Dude sues Best-O-Wax for specific performance of the contract. What result?

(A) Specific performance granted because the goods are unique.

(B) Specific performance granted because the replacement goods cost more.

(C) Specific performance denied because of the burden of enforcement.

(D) Specific performance denied because damages are adequate.

183. Princess Virginia obtains a cease and desist order against Photo Joe for his invasion of her privacy through the taking and printing of personal pictures. Joe fails to abide by the order, and continues to climb the trees near her castle in order to get exclusive photos with the use of his high-powered camera. Virginia files a motion to modify the injunction. What result?

(A) Denied because of the lack of changed circumstances.

(B) Denied because of Photo Joe's substantial and good faith compliance.

(C) Granted, and modified to require Joe to stay 25 feet away from Virginia's castle.

(D) Granted, and modified to prohibit Joe from printing any stories or pictures of Princess.

184. Tyson stole a painting from Potter's collection, mistakenly believing that the painting was a previously undiscovered Vermeer. In fact, the painting was an imitation by a lesser-known artist. At the time that Tyson stole the painting, the painting had a fair market value of $5000. Tyson sold the painting to an unsuspecting buyer for $1 million. What potential claims can Potter assert against Tyson? Which theory would be most advantageous to Potter?

ANSWER:

ANSWERS

1. **Answer (A) is the correct answer.** Although a specific remedy, replevin was a remedy traditionally available in the courts of law to a plaintiff in a case of conversion of goods or chattels.

   Answer (B) is incorrect. Specific performance is an equitable remedy available in a breach of contract case only if money damages and other forms of legal relief are inadequate.

   Answer (C) is incorrect. Constructive trust is an equitable remedy.

   Answer (D) is incorrect. Even though backpay involves the award of money to the plaintiff, courts have consistently characterized backpay as an equitable remedy.

2. A specific remedy grants the plaintiff the very object or benefit the plaintiff would have received had the defendant not committed the wrong. A substitutional remedy grants the plaintiff a benefit that is of equal value to the object or benefit lost as a result of the defendant's wrong.

3. **Answer (B) is the correct answer.** Even though both involve the award of money to the plaintiff, courts have consistently characterized backpay and frontpay as equitable remedies to which no right to a jury trial attaches.

   Answer (A) is incorrect. Plaintiff's amended complaint seeks only equitable relief. Thus, no right to a jury trial attaches. If Plaintiff's claims had raised mixed claims of law and equity, Plaintiff may have been entitled to a jury trial. In many jurisdictions, including the federal courts, Plaintiff would have a right to a jury trial on Plaintiff's legal claims if Plaintiff's case raised mixed claims of law and equity. However, in jurisdictions employing the "equitable clean-up" doctrine, Plaintiff may not have a right to a jury trial on legal claims if the court determines that the legal claims are ancillary to the equitable claims.

   Answer (C) is incorrect. The right to a jury trial attaches only to claims that arise at law. Even though Plaintiff seeks only monetary relief, courts have consistently characterized backpay and frontpay as equitable remedies to which no right to a jury trial attaches.

   Answer (D) is incorrect. Plaintiff's amended complaint seeks equitable relief only. If Plaintiff's claims had raised mixed claims of law and equity, Plaintiff may have been entitled to a jury trial. In many jurisdictions, including the federal courts, Plaintiff would have a right to a jury trial on Plaintiff's legal claims if Plaintiff's case raised mixed claims of law and equity. However, in jurisdictions employing the equitable clean-up doctrine, Plaintiff may not have a right to a jury trial on legal claims if the court determines that the legal claims are ancillary to the equitable claims.

4.   Potter can argue that the court should order Potter's reinstatement with backpay to effectuate the purposes of the Act. The Act is intended to prevent an employer from making employment decisions based on an employee's credit history. However, $500 in statutory damages is too minor a sanction to effectively deter an employer from violating the Act. Additionally, $500 and attorney fees is inadequate to compensate Potter for the harm suffered from the violation because Potter has lost his or her primary source of income. Conversely, Darko can argue that the statute provides express remedies and that the statutory language does not envision remedies in addition to those provided in the statute. Additionally, Darko can argue that the right created by the statute was unknown at common law, and as such, the statute should be strictly construed to preclude additional remedies.

5. **Answer (C) is the correct answer.** Under the Restatement (Second) of Contracts, the non-breaching party to a contract can recover the cost to remedy defects or complete performance if that cost is not clearly disproportionate to the loss in value to the non-breaching party. A court is most likely to award the cost to remedy a defect in performance even though it exceeds the loss in value to the owner where the defect frustrates the purpose of the contract. Here, the defect frustrates the purpose of the contract because the defect prevents Owner from using the prevailing winds to cool the building.

   Answer (A) is incorrect. Because the building has to be torn down and rebuilt, a substantial part of the cost to remedy the defect will consist of the cost to undo the defective performance. Where a large part of the cost to remedy the defect consists of the cost to undo the defective performance, courts generally will not award the cost to remedy. *See Jacob & Youngs v. Kent*, 230 N.Y. 239 (1921); Restatement (Second) Contracts § 348, cmt. c.

   Answer (B) is incorrect. Because this is an office building that Owner presumably holds for commercial rather than personal reasons, the aesthetic appearance of the office building is not likely central to the purpose of the contract. Therefore, the court would be unlikely to award the cost to remedy if it exceeds the diminished market value of the property.

   Answer (D) is incorrect. As discussed above, the court is likely to award the cost to remedy the defect under the circumstances described in **Answer (C).**

6. **Answer (B) is the correct answer.** Generally, the non-breaching party is entitled to recover its expectancy interest under the contract. Here, Benson's expectancy interest would be the profits Benson would have earned from operating the franchise. However, if a party cannot prove its expectancy with reasonable certainty, the party can recover as damages any expenses the non-breaching party incurred in reliance on or in furtherance of performance of the contract. Here, Benson likely cannot prove lost profits with reasonable certainty, because Benson has no previous restaurant experience on which to base an estimate of lost profits. Thus, Benson will be entitled to recover any expenses Benson incurred in performing the contract. Here, Benson incurred the advertising expenses in furtherance of performance under the franchise agreement, because the agreement required Benson to use best efforts to promote the franchise. Thus, Benson will be entitled to recover the advertising expenses.

Answer (A) is incorrect. To recover lost profits, Benson would have to prove past success in a sufficiently similar enterprise. Benson's success as an attorney is not sufficiently similar to be predictive of Benson's likely success as a restaurant owner.

Answer (C) is incorrect. Reliance damages are an alternative to expectancy damages and can be recovered only if the non-breaching party cannot establish its expectancy. Thus, Benson is entitled to recover either lost profits or the advertising fees but not both.

Answer (D) is incorrect. Even if Benson cannot prove the lost profits from the franchise with reasonable certainty, Benson will be able to establish the amount that Benson expended on advertising in reliance on the franchise agreement. Thus, Benson will be able to recover the advertising expenses as reliance damages.

7. **Answer (D) is the correct answer.** Special damages are those damages which do not flow necessarily and inherently from the breach but instead are caused by the particular needs of the non-breaching party. Generally, special damages are those that arise from the use of the object of the action rather than the injury or loss of the object itself. Under the Restatement (Second) of Torts, damages like the medical expenses in **Answer (A)** are considered special damages. Damages for loss of use of an automobile in **Answer (B)** are special damages. They are not damages to compensate for the actual damage to the vehicle. Instead, they are damages that arise from the owner's particular use of the automobile. Lost earnings in the defamation action in **Answer (C)** are also special damages. An injured party's specific lost earnings will depend on the particular individual's circumstances. Thus, all of the circumstances described in the problem are examples of special damages. **That result is found in Answer (D), making Answer (D) the correct answer and Answers (A), (B) and (C) incorrect.**

8. **Answer (B) is the correct answer.** In order to recover lost profits, the non-breaching party must make reasonable efforts to avoid lost profits and can only recover those portions of the lost profits which could not be avoided through reasonable efforts. The non-breaching party need not make extraordinary efforts to avoid the loss but need only take reasonable steps to avoid the loss. The reasonableness of the non-breaching party's efforts is determined by the individual circumstances of the non-beaching party. Here, because the sole proprietor is an individual, she may lack the means to locate a replacement truck in a different state or transport the replacement truck to the sole proprietor's home state. If so, she will be entitled to recover lost profits even though she did not purchase a replacement truck.

    Answer (A) is incorrect. The buyer failed to take reasonable efforts to avoid lost profits because the buyer could have purchased substitute component parts at a cheaper price than producing the components itself and, thereby avoided some of its lost profits.

    Answer (C) is incorrect. The farmer could have avoided lost profits by searching for a replacement tractor during the three months between the time of breach and the start of the planting system.

Answer (D) is incorrect. As discussed above, the sole proprietor in **Answer (B)** likely will be able to recover lost profits.

9.   Generally, comparative or contributory negligence applies to the plaintiff's actions or omissions before an accident occurs and which contribute to the injury. A failure to mitigate arises when the plaintiff fails to act after the accident in a manner that would have minimized or eliminated the plaintiff's injuries. One exception to this general rule is the failure to wear a seatbelt. Even though this failure occurs before an accident, some courts have considered the failure to wear a seatbelt to be a failure to mitigate damages.

10.   **Answer (C) is the correct answer.** A prevailing plaintiff is entitled to pre-judgment interest if the plaintiff's claim is liquidated or ascertainable. A claim is liquidated when damages will be computed by reference to an objective source or formula such as the fair market value of the automobile.

   Answer (A) is incorrect. Tort claims can be liquidated claims as long as damages are readily ascertainable, such as when damages will be based on an objective source or formula.

   Answer (B) is incorrect. A dispute over liability will not render a claim unliquidated.

   Answer (D) is incorrect. Parker will be entitled to pre-judgment interest only if Parker's fraud claim is a liquidated claim.

11.   **Answer (D) is the correct answer.** Post-judgment interest as distinguished from pre-judgment interest is interest that accrues from the date of judgment until the defendant satisfies the judgment. In most jurisdictions, it is awarded automatically by statute regardless of the nature of the claim.

   Answer (A) is incorrect. Post-judgment interest is awarded regardless of the legal theory under which the plaintiff sues.

   Answer (B) is incorrect. Post-judgment interest, unlike pre-judgment interest, is available even if a claim is unliquidated. Thus, post-judgment interest is available even if the amount of damages is committed to the discretion of the jury.

   Answer (C) is incorrect. Both pre-judgment and post-judgment interest are available if the defendant disputes liability.

12. **Answer (B) is the correct answer.** When a seller has wrongfully failed to deliver goods, Uniform Commercial Code (UCC) § 2-712 allows a buyer to "cover" by purchasing substitute goods and recover from the seller as damages the difference between the cost of cover and the contract price. However, the buyer's failure to cover does not preclude the buyer from recovering damages. Instead, under UCC § 2-713(a), a buyer is entitled to recover as damages the difference between the market price at the time for tender and the contract price. Here, Seller wrongfully failed to deliver 2000 widgets. Buyer has failed to cover. However, Buyer is entitled to recover damages under § 2-713(a). Buyer's damages will be measured as the difference between the market price at the time for tender which equals $8000 ($4.00 per widget × 2000 widgets) and the contract price of $2000 ($1.00 per widget × 2000 widgets). Thus, Buyer will be entitled to recover $6000. This result is found in **Answer (B)**, **making Answer (B) the correct answer** and **Answers (A), (C), and (D) incorrect answers.**

13. **Answer (A) is the correct answer.** When a buyer lawfully rejects non-conforming goods, UCC § 2-712 allows a buyer to "cover" by purchasing substitute goods and recover from the seller as damages the difference between the cost of cover and the contract price. Here, Bombay lawfully rejected non-conforming sprockets and purchased commercially reasonable substitute sprockets. Therefore, Bombay is entitled to recover damages under § 2-712. Bombay's damages will be measured as the difference between the cover price of $30,000 ($3.00 per sprocket wheel × 10,000 wheels) and the contract price of $10,000 ($1.00 per sprocket wheel × 10,000 wheels) or $20,000.

Answer (B) is incorrect. Bombay is entitled to recover the difference between the cost of cover and the contract price. Bombay is not entitled to recover the entire cost of cover.

Answer (C) is incorrect. Cover goods need only be reasonable substitutes. The fact that the cover goods cost more than the original goods by itself does not make the cover goods unreasonable substitutes. Indeed, by allowing the buyer to recover the difference between the cost of cover and the contract price, the UCC implicitly recognizes that commercially reasonable substitute goods may cost more than the original goods.

Answer (D) is incorrect. Bombay will not be entitled to recover *consequential* damages resulting from Bombay's intended use of the sprockets such as lost profits, because Bombay did not inform Super Sprockets of its intended use of the sprockets at the time of contracting. However, Bombay may recover its *general* damages. General damages are those damages that compensate Bombay for the loss of the actual object of the contract — here, the sprockets — rather than its use of that object. The law presumes that such losses are foreseeable to the seller. Here, the loss of the sprockets themselves will be measured as the difference between the cost of the cover sprockets and the contract price.

14. **Answer (B) is the correct answer.** Under UCC § 2-715, a buyer can recover consequential damages such as lost profits if those losses were foreseeable and unavoidable. Under the UCC, consequential damages must be foreseeable to the seller at the time of contracting. Consequential damages are foreseeable when the seller has reason to know of the particular needs of the buyer that cause the consequential loss. The UCC also requires the buyer to take reasonable steps through cover or otherwise to prevent the loss. If the loss occurs despite the buyer's reasonable efforts, the buyer can recover damages for the loss. Here, Betty's lost profits are consequential damages because they arise from Betty's intended use of the van. Betty has taken reasonable steps to avoid her lost profits by searching for a comparable van. Because no comparable van was available, her lost profits are unavoidable. However, Betty failed to communicate her intended use of the van to Stan until the time and place for delivery of the van. Thus, Stan had no reason to know of her intended use at the time of contracting and could not foresee her lost profits at the time of contracting. Accordingly, even though her lost profits are unavoidable, they were not foreseeable at the time of contracting, and hence, Betty is not entitled to recover damages for the lost profits. This result is found in **Answer (B)**, **making Answer (B) the correct answer** and **Answers (A), (C), and (D) incorrect answers.**

15. **Answer (C) is the correct answer.** Here, the contract is a mixed contract for goods and services. The contract obligated Electric Company to both deliver a good — the transformer — and perform a service — the installation of the transformer. While Electric Company performed its obligations by delivering a conforming transformer, Electric Company breached the contract by improperly installing the transformer. Metals Company is entitled to general damages for Electric Company's breach of the contract. These damages will be measured as the difference in the value of the installation as promised and the value of the installation as performed.

Answer (A) is incorrect. Under UCC § 2-714, the measure of damages when the buyer accepts non-conforming goods is the difference between the value of the goods as accepted and the value of the goods had the goods been delivered in the condition warranted by the seller.

Answer (B) is incorrect. Here, the transformer was delivered in the condition in which it was warranted. Thus, Metals Company received conforming goods. The harm to the transformer occurred as a result of Electric Company's negligent installation of the transformer. Thus, the harm to the transformer is a form of consequential damages. Ordinarily, the buyer would be entitled to recover consequential damages for the harm to the transformer. However, here the parties have expressly limited such damages in the contract. Thus, Metals Company is not entitled to recover damages for the harm to the transformer.

Answer (D) is incorrect. While Metals Company is entitled to general damages measured by the difference in value from the improper installation of the transformer, Metals Company is not entitled to consequential damages for the harm to the transformer because the contract expressly precludes such damages.

16. Simon is entitled to recover $0.02 per brick for the 200,000 bricks that Barbara rejected, or $4000. When a buyer refuses to accept conforming goods and the seller does not resell those goods, UCC § 2-708 provides that the seller is entitled to recover the difference between the contract price and the market price at the time and place for tender.

17. **Answer (B) is the correct answer.** Under UCC § 2-706, a seller is entitled to resell goods in a commercially reasonable manner and collect the difference between the resale price and the contract price. Here, because the greetings cards had a time-sensitive theme, Stone acted reasonably in attempting to sell the cards until Valentine's Day then waiting until the next Valentine's Day season to attempt a second resale.

    Answer (A) is incorrect. A seller such as Stone is entitled to recover price only if the goods are identified to the contract and cannot be resold through reasonable efforts. Here, the greeting cards were resold through reasonable albeit not immediate efforts.

    Answer (C) is incorrect. Given the seasonal nature of the greeting cards, Stone could reasonably wait until the appropriate season to attempt to resell the goods.

    Answer (D) is incorrect. Under UCC § 2-706, a seller such as Stone is entitled to resell goods at a private sale as long as the seller provides the buyer with reasonable notice of the resale.

18. **Answer (A) is the correct answer.** Under UCC § 2-706, a seller such as Stone is entitled to recover any incidental damages incurred as a result of the breach. Under UCC § 2-710, incidental damages include commercially reasonable expenses incurred in the care and custody of goods after the breach as well as expenses incurred in reselling the goods. Here, Stone incurred the rental fee in connection with the care and custody of the greeting cards after Brown's breach and so that Stone could resell the goods at an appropriate time. Further, Stone acted reasonably in storing the greeting cards until the appropriate season.

    Answer (B) is incorrect. A seller need not be successful in its resale efforts to recover expenses incurred in connection with the resale. The seller need only be reasonable in its efforts. Here, Stone acted reasonably in attempting to resell the greeting cards during the appropriate season, so Stone would be entitled to recover the rental fees even if Stone had not been able to resell the greeting cards.

Answer (C) is incorrect. While a seller such as Stone generally is precluded from recovering consequential losses, the rental fee is incidental to the contract between Stone and Brown rather than consequential because Stone incurred the rental fee in attempting to mitigate Stone's loss under the contract with Brown.

Answer (D) is incorrect. Stone need not inform Brown of the rental fees. Expenses incurred in attempting to mitigate the loss under the contract are presumed to be foreseeable to the breaching buyer.

19. **Answer (C) is the correct answer.** A lost volume seller is entitled to recover its profit under § 2-708(2).

    Answer (A) is incorrect. A seller may elect to recover the difference between the market value and the contract price. However, if that measure of damages would be inadequate, a seller may elect to recover its lost profits under UCC § 2-708(2). Here, if the standard retail price is less than the market value of the laptop computers, Super Computers may elect to recover the difference between the market value and the standard retail price. However, if the standard retail price is equal to or greater than the market value of the computers, this measure of recovery would be inadequate as it would yield no damages. Super Computers would not be precluded from recovering. Instead, it could recover its lost profits under UCC § 2-708(2).

    Answer (B) is incorrect. UCC § 2-708(2) allows a seller to recover its lost profits when market or resale damages would be inadequate. One of the circumstances under which § 2-708(2) applies is when the seller is a "lost volume seller." A lost volume seller is a seller who would have made a sale to a third party even if the original buyer had not breached. In other words, the seller would have made a sale to both the breaching party and the third party if the buyer had not breached. Under these circumstances, the seller has lost one sale and the profit on that one sale, even though the seller has resold the breaching buyer's goods.

    Answer (D) is incorrect. A lost volume seller is entitled to recover only its profits on the lost sale. The lost volume seller is not entitled to recover the entire contract price.

20. **Answer (D) is the correct answer.** Under UCC § 2-709, a seller is entitled to recover the price of the contracted-for goods under three circumstances: (1) if the buyer has accepted the goods; (2) if conforming goods are lost or damaged after the risk of loss has passed to the buyer; or (3) if the Buyer rejects conforming goods and the seller is unable to sell those goods after reasonable efforts. Thus, if Seller is not able to resell the molding machine, here, because it is designed for Buyer's specific uses, Seller will be entitled to recover the price of the molding machine. Likewise, if Buyer accepts delivery of the molding machine but refuses to pay for the molding machine, Seller will be entitled to recover price. Finally, because the contract requires Seller to ship the molding machine via common carrier but provides no express term allocating risk of loss while the goods are in the possession of the railroad, it is a shipment contract under the UCC. Under a shipment contract, the risk of loss passes to the buyer once the seller delivers

the goods to the carrier and makes a contract for their shipment. Here, Seller delivered the molding machine to the railroad and made a contract for its shipment before the molding machine was stolen. Thus, the risk of loss passed to Buyer before the molding machine was stolen. Hence, Seller is entitled to recover the price. As such, Seller is entitled to recover price under all three circumstances. This result is found in **Answer (D)**, **making Answer (D) the correct answer** and **Answers (A), (B), and (C) incorrect answers.**

21. Super Salty will be entitled to recover $1900. Super Salty will be entitled to recover the price of $500 ($5.00 per pound × 100 pounds) for the 100 pounds of processed nuts it completed. Under UCC § 2-709, a seller is entitled to recover price for goods identified to the contract that the seller is unable to resell through reasonable efforts. Here, Super Salty completed 100 pounds of processed nuts which are identified to the contract with Benny's Best. Super Salty was unable to resell the nuts because they were processed pursuant to Benny's Best's unique recipe. Super Salty also will be entitled to recover its lost profits for the remaining 400 pounds of nuts. UCC § 2-704 allows a seller that has not completed manufacturer of the contract goods prior to the breach to cease manufacturing if to do so would be commercially reasonable. Here, Super Salty acted reasonably in ceasing production, because no market appears to exist for the processed nuts. When a seller ceases production, market and resale differential damages will be inadequate. The measures envision that the seller will be able to resell finished goods. Thus, such a "components seller" is entitled to lost profits under § 2-708(2). Here, because Super Salty ceased production of the remaining 400 pounds of processed nuts, it has no finished goods. Accordingly, it is entitled to lost profits. Under UCC § 2-708(2), lost profits are measured as the seller's profits including reasonable overhead plus due allowance for costs reasonably incurred and less any payments or proceeds on resale. Profit is measured as the contract price less the seller's production costs. Here, Super Salty's anticipated profit was $2.00 per pound or $800 (($5.00 contract price – $2.00 cost of nuts – $0.50 cost of ingredients – $.050 cost of equipment and rent) × 400 pounds). The depreciation on its equipment and the rent on its plant would be considered overhead. Thus, assuming Super Salty's estimate of $0.50 per pound was reasonable, Super Salty will be entitled to recover $200 ($0.50 × 400 pounds) as well. Super Salty also is entitled to recover costs it has reasonably incurred. Here, Super Salty already has paid $800 for the 400 pounds of unprocessed nuts ($2.00 per pound × 400 pounds). Assuming Super Salty acted reasonably in purchasing the unprocessed nuts, it will be entitled to recover this cost as well. Finally, Super Salty's recovery will be reduced by any proceeds it received on resale of the components. Here, Super Salty was able to sell the unprocessed nuts for $400 ($1.00 per pounds × 400 pounds). Thus, Super Salty's recovery will be $1900 ($500 (price for completed nuts) + $800 (profit on unprocessed nuts) + $200 (overhead attributable to unfinished nuts) + $800 (costs incurred for unprocessed nuts) – $400 (profit earned on resale of unprocessed nuts)).

22. **Answer (C) is the correct answer.** Under the Restatement (Second) of Contracts, a court will uphold a liquidated damages provision if: (1) the damages resulting from a breach would be difficult to determine at the time the parties entered into the contract; and (2) the stipulated amount bears a reasonable relationship to either the anticipated or actual harm resulting from the breach. Here, if Contractor does not complete construction by the start of the school year, School District will be harmed in that it will have to find a new location to hold classes or re-configure existing facilities. This, in turn, could harm the educational experience of students who may be forced to attend classes in overcrowded facilities or move from one location to another during the course of the semester. The injury to the students' educational experience would be difficult to quantify. Moreover, the clause bears a reasonable relationship to the harm, because the rental value of comparable space is the most quantifiable measure of the harm.

Answer (A) is incorrect. The liquidated damages clause allows the shipper to recover the full contract price for goods that it does not have to ship and, hence, does not have to incur the costs of shipping. Thus, the clause provides for a greater recovery than either the actual or anticipated harm.

Answer (B) is incorrect. The harm to Landlord in the event of a breach likely will not be the loss of the entire rent. Rather, because Landlord can re-let the property, the harm is the difference between the rent due under the lease with Tenant and the fair rental value of the property. Here, the clause does not account for Landlord's ability to re-let the property. Thus, in the absence of evidence that Landlord would encounter difficulty in re-letting the property, the clause does not bear a reasonable relationship to the anticipated or actual harm.

Answer (D) is incorrect. Courts generally do not give controlling weight to the parties' characterization of the clause.

23. **Answer (C) is the correct answer.** Courts generally consider earnest money or down payment forfeiture clauses to be liquidated damages provisions that are presumptively valid. Courts will uphold such clauses unless the breaching party can show that the amount forfeited does not bear a reasonable relationship to the anticipated or actual harm to the seller. The actual harm to Smith would be the difference between the contract price and the market value or resale price of the condominium plus any consequential damages. If Brown can show that Smith could have resold the condominium for an amount significantly greater than $15,000 over the contract price, Brown likely can show that the forfeiture clause does not bear a reasonable relationship to Smith's actual or anticipated harm.

Answer (A) is incorrect. Most courts have abandoned the rule against allowing a breaching party to maintain an action for restitution.

Answer (B) is incorrect. Down payment or earnest money forfeiture clauses generally are considered liquidated damages clauses. The enforceability of such clauses does not turn on the willfulness of the breaching party.

Answer (D) is incorrect. Courts generally analyze forfeiture clauses as liquidated damages clauses and consider clauses that liquidate damages at 10 percent of the purchase price to be presumptively valid.

24. **Answer (A) is the correct answer.** Most courts adhere to the American rule. Under the American rule, a buyer such as Baker is entitled to recover full benefit of the bargain damages when a vendor such as Stone fails to deliver marketable title regardless of the reasons for the vendor's default. However, some jurisdictions adhere to the English rule. Under the English rule, when the vendor is unable to deliver marketable title through no fault of her own, a buyer's recovery is limited to the return of any purchase price paid and any expenses incurred in connection with the transaction. Here, if Stone was unaware of the easement, Stone will be without fault in the breach. Thus, Baker's recovery will be limited to the return of any purchase price paid in a jurisdiction that adheres to the English rule.

    Answer (B) is incorrect. While Baker's recovery will not be limited to restitution of purchase price in a jurisdiction that adheres to the American rule, Baker's recovery will be so limited in a jurisdiction that adheres to the English Rule. Thus, **Answer (A)** is preferable.

    Answer (C) is incorrect. Even under the more restrictive English rule, Baker will not be limited to restitution of purchase price and, instead, will be entitled to recover benefit of the bargain damages if Stone acted in bad faith.

    Answer (D) is incorrect. A buyer's compensatory damages are measured by the benefit that the buyer would have gained from the transaction, rather than the benefit that the seller would have gained from the transaction. This usually will be measured as the difference between the contract price and the fair market value of the property.

25. **Answer (D) is the correct answer.** Biggs was able to purchase a comparable home at a cheaper price and, hence, needed to borrow less money. However, Biggs still suffered harm, because Biggs had to take out a loan at a higher interest rate. As a result of the higher interest rate, Biggs ultimately will end up paying more for the second house than Biggs would have paid under the contract with Stanton. Under these circumstances, Biggs is entitled to recover the interest rate differential between the two loans. This would be measured by the difference between the total amount of interest and principal due under the $280,000 loan at 6% and the total amount of interest and principal due under the $270,000 loan at 7.5%. This result is found in **Answer (D), making Answer (D) the correct answer** and **Answers (A), (B), and (C) incorrect answers.**

26. **Answer (B) is the correct answer.** Penny is entitled to recover the reasonable value of any necessary medical services or treatments.

    Answer (A) is incorrect. Penny is entitled to recover the reasonable value of any necessary medical services regardless of whether she has paid for the services at the time of trial. The amount paid for the treatment may be offered as evidence to show the reasonable value of services. Likewise, the fact that Penny has paid for the treatment may be offered to show that the treatment was medically necessary.

    Answer (C) is incorrect. Penny can recover the reasonable value of necessary services even if the treating physician is unlicensed.

    Answer (D) is incorrect. Penny will be entitled to recover damages for her medical expenses regardless of whether her personal health insurance covers the loss. Indeed, under the collateral source rule, Dan will not be able to introduce into evidence the fact that Penny has insurance coverage for the losses. However, if Penny's insurance carrier has paid for her treatment, her insurance carrier may be entitled to recover from Penny any damages she receives from Dan.

27. **Answer (D) is the correct answer.** None of the circumstances provided will preclude an injured plaintiff from recovering damages for lost earning capacity.

    Answer (A) is incorrect. While damages for lost wages are awarded to compensate a plaintiff for wages lost from a specific job while the plaintiff was injured, lost earning capacity compensates a plaintiff for a decrease in her ability to work. Thus, lost earning capacity as distinguished from lost wages does not require a record of past earnings. As such, a child who has not yet entered the workforce can recover for lost earning capacity if she can demonstrate that she would have been able to earn more money over her worklife had she not been injured.

    Answer (B) is incorrect. A plaintiff who returns to her previous employment may recover for lost earning capacity if she can demonstrate that her opportunities for advancement, promotion or change of careers have been limited because of her injuries.

    Answer (C) is incorrect. A full-time care provider can recover for lost earning capacity if he can demonstrate that he would have been able to re-enter the workforce but is unable to do so or can do so only at a decreased salary because of his injuries. Alternatively, the full-time care provider may recover the replacement value of his child care services if he is unable to provide child care services as a result of his injuries.

28. A jury can consider numerous factors including the plaintiff's age, past employment history, education, training, opportunities for employment or promotion, and stated career intentions in determining the plaintiff's lost earning capacity.

29. **Answer (C) is the correct answer.** Awards that compensate for future pecuniary expenses that will recur periodically must be reduced to present value. Here, expenses for Peterman's daily nursing care will recur periodically after trial.

    Answer (A) is incorrect. Most courts agree that damages for pain and suffering need not be reduced to present value.

    Answer (B) is incorrect. Only damages for future pecuniary losses must be reduced to present value. Future losses are those that the plaintiff will incur after trial. While damages that compensate Peterman for the wages he lost before trial are damages for pecuniary losses, they compensate Peterman for past losses rather than future losses. Therefore, these damages do not need to be reduced to present value.

    Answer (D) is incorrect. While damages for Peterman's future daily nursing care must be reduced to present value, damages for lost wages need not be.

30. **Answer (D) is the correct answer.** In *Jones & Laughlin Steel Corp. v. Pfeifer*, 462 U.S. 523 (1983), the Supreme Court recognized that the discount rate should be based on the interest rate earned on "the best and safest" investment. The Court also recognized that inflation affects both the estimate of lost earnings and the discount rate and held that the discount rate should be chosen on the basis of the factors that are used to estimate the lost earnings. Essentially, inflation should be treated consistently on both sides of the equation. If inflation is excluded from estimates of lost wages, the inflation also should be excluded from the discount rate. Here, the method of discounting treats inflation consistently by including cost of living increases in the estimate of lost wages while using a market interest rate that reflects, in part, anticipated inflation. The discount rate also reflects the interest rate earned on reasonably safe investments, because triple A rated corporate bonds are reasonably safe investments.

    Answer (A) is incorrect. Here, the discount rate is based on the yield on junk bonds. Junk bonds are not reasonably safe investments. Additionally, inflation has been excluded from the estimate of lost wages because the estimate excludes increases due to the cost of living. However, inflation has been factored into the discount rate because the discount rate uses a market interest rate.

    Answer (B) is incorrect. The yield on triple A rated corporate bonds reflects an interest rate earned on reasonably safe investments. However, the method treats inflation inconsistently between the estimate of lost earnings and the discount rate. The estimate of lost earnings excludes any increase in earnings due to inflation because it excludes cost-of-living increases. However, the discount rate includes an estimate of inflation. The current market yield on triple A rated corporate bonds reflects, in part, a predicted inflation rate. The yield is increased to account for anticipated price inflation before the bond's maturity. Thus, this method of discounting runs the risk of undercompensating Peterson.

Answer (C) is incorrect. This method of discounting treats inflation consistently by including cost of living increases in the estimate of lost wages while using a market interest rate that reflects, in part, anticipated inflation. However, a junk bond is not a reasonably safe investment.

31. A plaintiff can recover damages for any noneconomic harms resulting from the defendant's misconduct, including pain and suffering, loss of enjoyment of life, mental and physical anguish and disfigurement. Some jurisdictions treat each of these claims as a separate item of recovery, while other jurisdiction treat these all as components of pain and suffering.

32. **Answer (A) is the correct answer.** Patty received medical services, so she will be entitled to recover the reasonable value of those services, provided that they were medically necessary. While Patty also received the benefit of her Aunt's gratuitous services, she received that benefit from her Aunt who has no relationship to the defendant. Thus, under the collateral source rule, the defendant will not be entitled to offset the harm and the benefit.

Answer (B) is incorrect. The plaintiff is entitled to recover the entire reasonable value of medical services provided.

Answer (C) is incorrect. Generally, the defendant's state of mind does not affect the plaintiff's entitlement to compensatory damages. The defendant's state of mind, however, will affect the plaintiff's ability to recover punitive damages.

Answer (D) is incorrect. Patty received a benefit when her Aunt provided the medical services gratuitously. However, that benefit was collateral to the defendant's misconduct. Thus, under the collateral source rule, the defendant will not be entitled to offset the harm and the benefit.

33. **Answer (C) is the correct answer.** An injured party must undergo reasonable treatment that is within her means. An injured party need not endure undue hardships, including financial hardships, to avoid a loss. If Pierson lacks the financial means to pay for the surgery, she will be entitled to recover damages for her pain and suffering.

Answer (A) is incorrect. While a defendant must take the plaintiff as the defendant finds her, the plaintiff has a duty to use reasonable and proper efforts to minimize harm and restore herself. The defendant is not required to compensate the plaintiff for harm that could be avoided through reasonable means. Here, surgery could alleviate Pierson's pain and suffering. Thus, Pierson will have a duty to undertake the surgery if a reasonable person would undergo the surgery, and Davidson will not have to pay damages for the pain and suffering that could be alleviated by the surgery if Pierson refuses to undergo the surgery.

Answer (B) is incorrect. Pierson must undertake all reasonable steps to avoid her pain and suffering. A reasonable person might undertake the surgery if it involved only a slight risk of failure.

Answer (D) is incorrect. Pierson need only undergo those treatments to which a reasonable person would submit. If a reasonable person would not undergo the corrective surgery, Pierson will be entitled to recover her full pain and suffering damages.

34.   **Answer (B) is the correct answer.** A spouse such as Wilma is entitled to maintain an action for loss of consortium. However, a spouse's consortium recovery cannot be duplicative of the injured party's recovery. Wilma will be entitled to recover damages for her loss of consortium. Her damages for her noneconomic losses such as her loss of companionship will not be duplicative of Harrison's recovery, because she suffers a separate and distinct loss.

       Answer (A) is incorrect. Here, if Harrison recovers damages for his lost wages, Wilma cannot recover damages for her loss of financial support from Harrison because these damages would be duplicative of the damages for lost wages.

       Answer (C) is incorrect. Recovery for loss of financial support would be duplicative of Harrison's recovery for lost wages.

       Answer (D) is incorrect. Wilma will be entitled to maintain an action for loss of consortium and recover any damages that are not duplicative of Harrison's damages.

35.   **Answer (B) is the correct answer.** A spouse's claim for loss of consortium is derivative of the injured party's claim. As such, a claim for loss of consortium is barred or reduced in the same manner as the injured spouse's recovery. Here, Harrison's recovery will be reduced proportionally to his fault, so Wilma's recovery will be likewise reduced.

       Answer (A) is incorrect. Wilma's recovery will be reduced in the same manner as Harrison's recovery. In a comparative fault jurisdiction, Harrison's recovery will be reduced by the percentage at which he is at fault rather than barred. Thus, Wilma's recovery will be reduced proportionally rather than precluded.

       Answer (C) is incorrect. Loss of consortium protects the marital relationship from acts of third parties only. It does not give the non-injured spouse a right to recovery from the injured spouse.

       Answer (D) is incorrect. Because Wilma's loss of consortium claim is derivative of Harrison's personal injury claim her recovery will be reduced in the same manner as Harrison's recovery.

36.   **Answer (B) is the correct answer.** Traditionally, a plaintiff must maintain a single action for all past, present and future losses arising from a single transaction or occurrence. A plaintiff may recover damages for future losses only if the plaintiff demonstrates that those future losses are reasonably certain to occur. Here, Poppins

must maintain a single action to recover damages for her injuries both from the burns and the potential cancer in a single action because they arise from a single occurrence. She can recover damages relating to future treatment for cancer if she proves with reasonable certainty that she is likely to develop cancer.

Answer (A) is incorrect. Generally, courts have permitted plaintiffs to recover damages for an increased fear of future harms such as cancer if the plaintiffs are unable to prove to a reasonable certainty that they will incur the likely harm. However, the increased fear of future harm is a present harm rather than a future harm. The plaintiff suffers from a fear of future harm as soon as the exposure occurs. Thus, the plaintiff need not prove to a reasonable certainty that some future harm will occur. Instead, the plaintiff must show that her current fear is reasonable.

Answer (C) is incorrect. Generally, res judicata precludes a plaintiff from splitting her cause of action. Instead, she must file a single cause of action to recover damages for all of her injuries arising from a single transaction or occurrence. Here, if Poppins files an action to recover damages for injuries relating to the burns, she will be precluded from filing a second action to recover damages for her treatment for cancer because both injuries arise from the same occurrence.

Answer (D) is incorrect. A stated above, a plaintiff can recover for future losses as long as she proves those losses to a reasonable certainty.

37.   **Answer (A) is the correct answer.** Most states now provide by statute that causes of action survive the victim's death. Under these survival statutes, an estate, like Watson's Estate, can maintain an action against a tortfeasor and collect any damages to which the victim would have been entitled had the victim survived.

Answer (B) is incorrect. Most states now have created by statute a claim for wrongful death. The wrongful death claim allows specified beneficiaries to recover damages they suffer as a result of the victim's death. However, here, Watson's Beneficiaries would not have a wrongful death claim against Davis because Davis did not cause Watson's death.

Answer (C) is incorrect. Watson's beneficiaries do not have a wrongful death claim against Davis because Davis did not cause Watson's death.

Answer (D) is incorrect. States generally allow the victim's tort claim to survive her death and also allow specified beneficiaries to pursue a claim for wrongful death.

38.   **Answer (C) is the correct answer.** Generally, an estate can recover damages only for wages lost between the time of injury and the time of death and cannot recover damages for lost future wages or future lost earning capacity. However, the beneficiaries of the decedent can recover damages for the loss of the financial support that the decedent would have provided had the decedent survived.

Answer (A) is incorrect. Generally, the estate can recover damages only for past lost wages measured as the wages the decedent lost from the time of injury until death.

Answer (B) is incorrect. Allowing Parker's Estate to recover for lost future wages and Parker's beneficiaries to recover for lost financial support would result in an impermissible duplicative recovery. Had Parker survived, the financial support to Parker's beneficiaries would have come from these future wages.

Answer (D) is incorrect. Generally, the estate can recover damages for wages lost between injury and death.

39. **Answer (B) is the correct answer.** Most courts now recognize a claim for wrongful pregnancy. The trend is to limit recovery to damages for the pregnancy itself, including medical expenses, lost wages and pain and suffering from labor and delivery. However, courts have allowed claims for child-rearing expenses when the child is born with a disability.

Answer (A) is incorrect. The Pattersons do have a claim for wrongful pregnancy rather than wrongful birth. However, the trend is to reject claims for child-rearing expenses unless the baby is born with a disability. Thus, the Pattersons are not likely to recover their child-rearing expenses unless the baby was born with a disability.

Answer (C) is incorrect. Courts generally have allowed claims for child-rearing expenses when a child is born with a disability.

Answer (D) is incorrect. The avoidable consequences rule only requires the injured party to take reasonable steps to avoid her loss. Requiring a parent to place a child up for adoption would impose an unreasonable burden on the parent. *See Smith v. Gore*, 728 S.W.2d 738, 751-52 (Tenn. 1987).

40. **Answer (A) is the correct answer.** The statute caps damages at the greater of $250,000 or three times economic damages. However, it also further caps damages at a maximum of $350,000 per plaintiff and $500,000 per occurrence. Here, Wendy was awarded $750,000 in economic damages ($250,000 in lost wages + $500,000 in medical expenses). Wendy was awarded $1 million in noneconomic damages (pain and suffering). Harold was awarded $500,000 in noneconomic damages because all of his loss of consortium damages where awarded to compensate for noneconomic losses. Thus, Wendy and Harold were awarded a combined total of $1.5 million in noneconomic damages. Neither Wendy's nor Harold's noneconomic damages exceed three times Wendy's economic damages or $2.25 million. However, both awards exceed the $350,000 limit for each plaintiff. Further, reducing both awards to $350,000 would exceed the $500,000 per occurrence cap. Both awards stem from a single occurrence because both arise from Wendy's use of the defective product. Thus, their combined total even if reduced to $350,000 per plaintiff would exceed the occurrence limit. As such, Wendy and Harold are entitled to a combined award of $500,00 for noneconomic damages, and the jury verdict must be reduced by $1 million to $1.25 million. **This result is found in Answer (A), making Answer (A) the correct answer and Answers (B), (C) and (D) incorrect.**

41.   Hewlett is likely to recover either the $560 pre-tort value of the jalopy or the $60 diminution in value as damages. Hewlett is not likely to recover the cost to repair the jalopy. Generally, courts allow an injured plaintiff to recover the cost to repair damaged property if repairs are both physically and economically feasible. Courts differ as to at what point repairs become economically infeasible. For some courts, repairs become economically infeasible when the cost to repair exceeds the diminution in value to the property. For others, the repairs become economically infeasible when the cost to repair exceeds the pre-tort value. Here, the cost to repair the jalopy exceeds both the $60 diminution in value and the $560 pre-tort value of the jalopy. Thus, Hewlett will not recover the cost to repair under either standard and will recover either $560 or $60 in damages depending on which standard the court applies.

42.   **Answer (A) is the correct answer.** Most jurisdictions permit a plaintiff to recover both for the physical damage to property and for the economic loss of the use of the property when property is destroyed. When property is destroyed, the pre-tort market value of the property compensates the plaintiff for the physical injury to the property only. The plaintiff is also entitled to damages for loss of use. However, the plaintiff's damages for loss of use are limited by the duty to mitigate. Thus, the plaintiff can recover damages for loss of use only for that period of time reasonably necessary to replace the destroyed property.

    Answer (B) is incorrect. A plaintiff is entitled to recover damages for loss of use regardless of whether the plaintiff's use of the property was commercial or personal.

    Answer (C) is incorrect. Historically, courts prohibited plaintiffs from recovering loss of use damages for destroyed goods under the theory that the market value of the goods encompassed the right to use the goods. However, most courts now recognize that damages paid to allow the plaintiff to purchase a replacement good, such as the pre-tort market value of the good, do not compensate the plaintiff for the economic loss resulting from the loss of the use of the good while the plaintiff seeks a replacement.

    Answer (D) is incorrect. The plaintiff's total recovery is not capped at the pre-tort value of the good.

43.   **Answer (C) is the correct answer.** When a plaintiff has lost goods that fluctuate in value, most jurisdictions follow the "New York rule." The New York rule allows the plaintiff to recover the highest value of the property between the time the plaintiff learns of conversion and the expiration of a reasonable time after the person learns of the conversion. A reasonable time after the conversion is measured by the time in which it

would take a reasonable person with adequate funds to replace the converted goods. Here, Client learned of the conversion on June 1, so Client would be entitled to the highest market value of the stock between June 1 and a reasonable time in which to replace the stock. Because stock can be traded relatively easily and quickly, a reasonable investor likely would have replaced the stock by July 1. The highest price between June 1 and July 1 appears to be $110 per share.

Answer (A) is incorrect. When goods fluctuate in value, most jurisdictions would not limit the plaintiff's recovery to the market price at the time of conversion.

Answer (B) is incorrect. Under the New York rule, the court disregards the market value of the goods between the time of conversion and the time the plaintiff learns of the breach under the theory that if the plaintiff had intended to sell the goods during this period of time, the plaintiff would have learned of the breach sooner.

Answer (D) is incorrect. While the plaintiff has no obligation to replace the converted goods, the plaintiff's recovery is limited to those losses that the plaintiff could not reasonably avoid through cover. Thus, under the New York rule, the plaintiff's recovery is limited to the highest value of the goods between the time the plaintiff learns of the conversion and the reasonable period in which to purchase replacement goods.

44. **Answer (D) is the correct answer.** When clothing and other household items are lost or destroyed, the owner is entitled to recover the actual value of the goods to the owner. In determining the actual value, the trier of fact is to consider the original purchase price, the replacement cost and the age, wear and condition of the goods at the time they were destroyed or lost.

Answer (A) is incorrect. The owner is awarded the actual value to the owner rather than the market value for two reasons. First, the market value of goods such as used clothing is difficult to ascertain. Second, the market value for used clothing does not adequately compensate the owner because the owner is unlikely to replace the lost goods with used or second hand goods.

Answer (B) is incorrect. While the cost to replace the clothing is a factor for the trier of fact to consider, it is not dispositive. Instead, the owner is entitled to the actual value of goods to the owner. Actual value is measured by several factors in addition to the cost to replace.

Answer (C) is incorrect. As with the cost to replace the clothing, the original purchase price is one of the factors for the trier of fact to consider in determining the actual value of the goods to the owner. However, it is not dispositive.

45. **Answer (A) is the correct answer.** An owner is permitted to offer personal testimony as to the value even though not an expert. However, the owner must provide some basis for the opinion other than mere speculation.

Answer (B) is incorrect. Palmer may explain through testimony how he arrived at his opinion as to value. He need not provide supporting documentation.

Answer (C) is incorrect. Even if Palmer is not otherwise an expert in clothing, he is entitled to offer opinion testimony about the value of his own belongings.

Answer (D) is incorrect. A plaintiff need not offer expert testimony as to value. Instead, Palmer may offer his own testimony as to value as long as he also explains his basis for arriving at that value.

46. **Answer (B) is the correct answer.** When property that derives its primary value from sentiment is destroyed, most courts allow the owner to recover the actual value to the owner. However, most courts exclude any consideration of sentimental or emotional value from the measure of actual value. Instead, actual value includes factors such as the cost to replace and the original purchase price. Here, the photograph holds primarily sentimental value for Palmer. Thus, Palmer will be entitled to recover the actual value. However, the jury will be prohibited from considering Palmer's sentimental attachment to the photograph and, instead, will be limited to considering the cost to purchase the film and develop the photograph. The market value of comparable goods may be relevant. However, to be relevant, the market value must be the market value of truly comparable goods. Here, the informal snapshot taken by Palmer's friend is not comparable to professional photographs of the rock star sold to magazines and newspapers. Thus, evidence of their market value likely is not relevant. As such, only the cost of purchasing and developing the film are likely to be considered by the jury. **This result is found in Answer (B), making Answer (B) the correct answer and Answers (A), (C) and (D) incorrect.**

47. If LaSalle Realty does not recover the cost to repair its building, it will not be put in the position it enjoyed prior to Outdoor Advertising's improper conduct. Before Outdoor Advertising installed the sign, LaSalle Realty held real property worth $2 million. If awarded the diminution in value rather than the cost to repair as damages, after Outdoor Advertising's misconduct, LaSalle Realty would hold $2 million in assets. However, LaSalle Realty would hold real property worth only $1.8 million. If LaSalle Realty wished to hold $2 million in real property or wished to hold this particular piece of real property, LaSalle Realty would have to pay the cost to repair the building out of its own pocket or LaSalle Realty would have to sell the building and combine the proceeds from the sale with the damage award to purchase a new $2 million building. This would be particularly inadequate given that real property is considered unique. On the other hand, if LaSalle Realty recovers repair costs in excess of the diminution in value, it may be overcompensated. If LaSalle Realty were to sell the building without making the repairs, the repair costs combined with the sale proceeds would exceed the original fair market value of the building. Thus, LaSalle Realty would reap a windfall. This may be particularly true where a landowner such as LaSalle Realty holds the property for commercial purposes only.

48. **Answer (D) is the correct answer.** Under the Restatement (Second) of Torts § 929 and the accompanying commentary, a landowner is entitled to recover the cost to repair an injury to her land unless that repair cost is disproportionate to the diminution in value. Even when the repair cost is disproportionate to the diminution in value, the owner can recover reasonable repair costs if the owner has a reason personal to the owner for repairing the land. Courts and commentators have interpreted this to mean that the owner must have a particular reason for restoring the land and that reason must be objectively reasonable. Here, the landowner in Answer (A) is entitled to the cost to repair the sand dune because it does not exceed the diminution in value to the land. Both the homeowner in Answer (B) and the church in Answer (C) are entitled to recover the cost to repair, even though the repair costs exceed the diminution in value because both have objectively reasonable particular reasons for restoring the land. Thus, all three cases support the award of repair costs. **This result is found in Answer (D), making Answer (D) the correct answer and Answers (A), (B) and (C) incorrect.**

49. **Answer (D) is the correct answer.** At common law, when a tree was wrongfully destroyed or removed from a landowner's property, the landowner was entitled to only the market value at the time of removal even if the tree had not yet reached its commercial maturity. Because this measure might undercompensate the landowner who would have otherwise raised the tree to commercial maturity and harvested it at that time, many states have enacted timber trespass statutes that allow a landowner to recover treble damages from a defendant who maliciously, intentionally or willfully removes or destroys a tree.

     Answer (A) is incorrect. Generally, when a tree is wrongfully destroyed or removed from a landowner's property, the landowner's recovery is limited to the market value at the time of removal even if the tree has not yet reached its commercial maturity. Any other measure might overcompensate the landowner and would be speculative.

     Answer (B) is incorrect. Awarding the current market value for mature trees might overcompensate the injured landowner and is speculative. Loud has saved the expense of growing the walnut trees to maturity. Further, Loud may begin re-generating the land sooner than he would have been able to had he grown the walnut trees to maturity. Finally, even if Bunyan had not removed the walnut trees, the trees could have died before they reached maturity or the market price could have dropped before the trees reached maturity.

     Answer (C) is incorrect. Generally, when a tree with commercial value is removed from the landowner's property, the landowner is entitled to the market value at the time of removal rather than the cost to replace the tree.

50. **Answer (A) is the correct answer.** Generally, when shrubs or trees without market value are removed or destroyed, the landowner is entitled to recover only the diminution in value to the land as a result of their destruction because the cost to replace the trees likely exceeds the diminution in value.

Answer (B) is incorrect. The landowner likely cannot recover the cost to replace the trees because the cost to replace the trees generally exceeds the diminution in value and because awarding the cost to replace when it exceeds the diminution in value would result in economic waste or a windfall to the landowner.

Answer (C) is incorrect. The original purchase price is not an accurate measure of the harm caused by the later destruction of the property.

Answer (D) is incorrect. A landowner is entitled to recover damages for the destruction of property even if the property has no marketable use.

51. **Answer (B) is the correct answer.** Punitive damages are imposed on a defendant who has engaged in serious misconduct with a bad state of mind. Generally, a defendant must act maliciously, oppressively, wantonly or at least recklessly. Here, the fact that Dirk drove his car into Peterson's house for revenge suggests that Dirk acted intentionally to cause harm to Peterson's house. This, in turn, suggests that Dirk acted maliciously.

    Answer (A) is incorrect. Punitive damages are imposed to punish a defendant for a limited type of misconduct—serious misconduct undertaken with a bad state of mind. A defendant generally must intend to cause harm to the plaintiff or at least act recklessly in the sense that defendant consciously disregard the risk of harm to the plaintiff. Here, while Dirk acted wrongfully in driving while his license was suspended, the act of driving with a suspended license does not demonstrate that Dirk intended to harm Peterson's house or even that Dirk acted recklessly in consciously disregarding a risk of harm to Peterson's house.

    Answer (C) is incorrect. As discussed above, **Answer (A)** would not support the imposition of punitive damages.

    Answer (D) is incorrect. An invasion of only economic rights can rise to the requisite level of misconduct as long as the invasion is sufficiently serious and the defendant acts with the requisite state of mind.

52. Punitive damages are imposed primarily to punish a defendant and to deter the defendant and others from engaging in similar misconduct. Some courts and commentators have recognized some additional non-compensatory functions such as financing the cost of litigation.

53. **Answer (B) is the correct answer.** Although punitive damages are not available in breach of contract cases, punitive damages may be awarded if the conduct constituting a breach of contract also constitutes an independent tort. Bad faith denial of insurance coverage constitutes an independent tort. Therefore, Palmer may be entitled to punitive damages if Palmer succeeds on the bad faith claim.

    Answer (A) is incorrect. Punitive damages are not available for breach of contract claims.

    Answer (C) is incorrect. Punitive damages are not available for breach of contract claims.

Answer (D) is incorrect. Punitive damages are available in claims involving a contractual relationship if the facts constituting breach of contract also constitute an independent tort.

54.   **Answer (C) is the correct answer.** In most states, a principal such as Big-Mart can be held vicariously liable for punitive damages based on the acts of its agent under two circumstances: (1) if the principal authorized, participated in or ratified the agent's conduct; or (2) if the agent was employed in a managerial capacity. A few states allow a principal to be held vicariously liable for punitive damages based on the acts of its agent so long as the agent acted within the scope of her authority. Under either test, Big-Mart can be held liable either if the employee at issue acted in a managerial capacity or if Big-Mart managers were aware of the practice and failed to stop it. This would demonstrate that the managers condoned or ratified the practice.

Answer (A) is incorrect because it is underinclusive. While Big-Mart may be held vicariously liable if its managers were aware of the discriminatory practice, it also may be held liable if the employee at issue was a manager.

Answer (B) is incorrect because it is underinclusive. While Big-Mart may be held vicariously liable if the employee at issue was a manager, it also may be held liable if its managers were aware of the discriminatory practice and failed to stop it.

Answer (D) is incorrect. As discussed above, employers may be held vicariously liable for punitive damages based on the acts of their employees.

55.   **Answer (B) is the correct answer.** Most jurisdictions allow punitive damages for "reckless indifference" or "gross negligence." Under either formulation, jurisdictions allow punitive damages in a products liability action if the defendant had actual knowledge of a defect and acted in bad faith by marketing the product without correcting the known defect or failing to warn consumers of the defect. Here, Neptune had actual knowledge of the defect through its internal testing data and acted in bad faith by marketing the car without taking steps to correct the defect.

Answer (A) is incorrect. While Neptune may be liable for punitive damages if it has engaged in intentional misconduct, intentional misconduct is not necessary. As discussed above, Neptune may be liable for punitive damages if it has acted with reckless indifference or gross negligence.

Answer (C) is incorrect. To be liable for punitive damages, a defendant must engage in something more than simple negligence. In the products liability context, this requires that the defendant have actual knowledge of the defect. Failure to detect a defect is insufficient.

Answer (D) is incorrect. As discussed above, Neptune will not be liable for punitive damages if it has been merely negligent.

56. **Answer (D) is the correct answer.** Most states permit a jury to consider a defendant's net wealth or financial condition under the theory that a sanction must be greater to punish a wealthy defendant than a poor defendant. The use of financial condition or net wealth has been subject to much criticism recently, including by the Supreme Court. However, the Supreme Court has not prohibited the use of net wealth as a factor, and most courts continue to permit juries to consider net wealth. Indeed, one state, California, has mandated that juries must consider net wealth in determining the size of a punitive damage award. Perhaps more controversial is the consideration of the plaintiff's litigation costs. Punitive damages are imposed to punish the defendant and deter the defendant and others from engaging in similar misconduct. The plaintiff's litigation costs would seem to have no relationship to these two goals. However, some commentators have recognized financing litigation as an ancillary goal of punitive damages. Additionally, some commentators have justified consideration of litigation costs on deterrence grounds. Awarding litigation costs increases the likelihood that a plaintiff will bring suit. Increasing the likelihood that a plaintiff will bring suit, in turn, deters a defendant from engaging in misconduct. Finally, most states permit a jury to consider the extent of the plaintiff's harm on the ground that the extent of the plaintiff's harm is one indicator of the gravity of the defendant's misconduct. Thus, all of the listed factors are appropriate for a jury to consider in determining an award of punitive damages. Indeed, each factor has been utilized in at least one state. **This result is found in Answer (D), making Answer (D) the correct Answer and Answers (A), (B) and (C) incorrect.**

57. The Court identified three guideposts that indicated that the award in *BMW v. Gore* was grossly excessive: (1) the degree of reprehensibility; (2) the ratio of punitive damages to the amount of harm inflicted on the plaintiff; and (3) the comparison between the punitive damage award and civil and criminal sanctions for comparable misconduct.

58. **Answer (C) is the correct answer.** In *State Farm v. Campbell*, 538 U.S. 408 (2003), the Supreme Court created a presumption against the constitutionality of a punitive damage award that exceeds a single-digit ratio of punitive to compensatory damages. However, the Court also recognized that awards in which the ratio is greater than 9-to-1 may comport with due process if the defendant engages in particularly egregious conduct that results in only slight economic harm. Here, Hospitality Inn has engaged in egregious conduct by knowingly letting guests rooms infested with bedbugs. However, its conduct has produced only slight economic harm. A greater award can be justified here on the grounds that such an award is necessary to prevent the defendant from profiting from its conduct and to encourage victims to bring suit and, hence, deter the defendant from engaging in the misconduct. *See Mathias v. Accor Economy Lodging*, 347 F.3d 672 (7th Cir. 2003).

    Answer (A) is incorrect. While the *State Farm* Court recognized that awards exceeding a single-digit ratio rarely comport with due process, the Court did not set up an irrebuttable presumption. Instead, the Court recognized that awards in which the ratio is greater than 9-to-1 may comport with due process if the defendant engages in particularly egregious conduct that results in only slight economic harm.

Answer (B) is incorrect. While Pittman suffered only slight economic injuries, other guests appear to have suffered greater economic injuries as a result of their severe physical injuries. Because they have suffered greater economic injuries, they presumably have greater incentive to sue and are more likely to recover significant compensatory damages, thereby providing an effective deterrent to the defendant's misconduct.

Answer (D) is incorrect. In *State Farm*, the Court recognized that a punitive damage award in a case based on unrelated or dissimilar misconduct could not provide the basis for an increased punitive award.

59. In most jurisdictions, Peters will be entitled to punitive damages because Officer acted with the requisite state of mind by acting knowingly and intentionally and because Peters suffered actual damage as evidenced by the award of nominal damages. A minority of jurisdictions require an injured party to show not only actual harm but also compensatory harm to be entitled to punitive damages. In those jurisdictions, Peters would not be entitled to punitive damages because the jury found that Peters had suffered no compensable harm and, hence, failed to award any compensatory damages.

60. **Answer (C) is the correct answer.** The irreparable injury rule requires that a plaintiff establish that her legal injury cannot adequately be remedied by damages. Irreparable injury is established where damages are difficult to measure, where the subject of a contract is unique, or where intangible or personal harm is threatened. The rule establishes the doctrinal line between remedies at law and equity, which historically were awarded by different courts with separate jurisdiction.

    Answer (A) is incorrect. A mere legal injury is insufficient to establish a qualification for injunctive relief. Legal injury is required before any remedy may be imposed by a court. The preference is to award damages for that legal injury unless a plaintiff establishes irreparable injury where legal remedies are inadequate.

    Answer (B) is incorrect. Injury in fact is necessary for a plaintiff to establish standing to bring a case. Injury in fact must also be established by the evidence in order to entitle the plaintiff to any remedy. However, the mere existence of a factual injury is insufficient to qualify for an injunction.

    Answer (D) is incorrect because the law doctrinally requires more than a plaintiff's choice to issue an injunction. The courts' preference is to award a final damages remedy rather than a prospective injunctive remedy. Thus, more than the plaintiff's desire is required before a court will issue an injunction.

61. **Answer (B) is the correct answer.** Specific performance of a contract is available where the subject of the contract is unique and cannot easily be replaced on the market. Here, the uniqueness and rarity of the soccer team itself makes it difficult to replace the team on the market. Also, the damage to the civic pride and reputation of the city as a result of the loss of the team would be difficult to measure.

    Answer (A) is incorrect. Specific performance is not always available for breach of contract. Only where the subject of the contract is unique, difficult to replace on the market, or where damages are difficult to measure will the equitable remedy be awarded. Where such uniqueness or difficulty is missing, the contractual party is limited to the remedy of damages.

    Answer (C) is incorrect because the burden of supervision on the court is not any more difficult than a routine injunction, as the court will just monitor whether the Aquas play their home games in Municipal Stadium.

    Answer (D) is incorrect. The public policy or public interest against the issuance of an injunction is relevant, but must be significant to outweigh the plaintiff's request for a particular injunction. Here, while law and economics scholars favor efficient breaches of contract, the law permits specific performance to enforce contractual promises where damages are inadequate or the subject of the contract is unique.

62. Poseidon's best argument against the issuance of the injunction is that the balance of the hardships weighs against the plaintiff's request for an injunction. First, Poseidon can argue that the City's loss of the leasing team can easily be replaced by monetary damages measured by the amount remaining to be paid on the lease plus any incidental losses to the City. Second, Poseidon will argue that the livelihood and continued existence of the team depend upon his ability to make a profit. Forcing a business to close or go out of business would impose an undue hardship upon a defendant sufficient to outweigh the plaintiff's irreparable injury. Finally, Poseidon might argue that public policy in favor of free market competition favors the denial of the injunction so that the team might breach an inefficient contract and maximize profits through the citizens of Treasure Island.

63. **Answer (A) is the correct answer.** The undue hardship on Perfumania outweighs the harm to plaintiffs. Closing down the factory causes tremendous economic waste by abandoning a factory that produces an economic good, includes significant capital investment, and employs hundreds of people. In addition, plaintiffs' harm is mere annoyance rather than harm to physical health. Where such economic waste outweighs plaintiffs' harm, an injunction will not be granted and plaintiffs will be awarded compensatory damages.

    Answer (B) is incorrect because there is no undue burden on the court from shutting down the plant as the order would be a simple, negative injunction that would require no ongoing monitoring or necessary oversight.

    Answer (C) is incorrect because the balance of the hardships, given the defendant's substantial economic waste, tip in favor of defendant, not plaintiff.

    Answer (D) is incorrect because even if the neighbors are able to establish irreparable injury, that injury is outweighed by the undue burden to the defendant. The neighbors might successfully argue irreparable injury because their emotional distress, annoyance and lack of enjoyment of property are intangible and difficult to measure. However, the plaintiffs' irreparable injury is outweighed by the significant undue hardship to the defendant discussed in Answer A so that the injunction will be denied.

64. **Answer (B) is the correct answer.** A prerequisite for issuing injunctions is a real threat of imminent harm. Here, the fears of the neighbors are subjective and do not establish a real threat. Moreover, there is no "legal" harm threatened since the building, traffic, and residents are not per se violative of the law. It is only if those things later rise to a level of a legal nuisance that the Nimbes would have an actionable claim at law.

    For this reason, **Answer (A) is incorrect,** since there is no legal harm threatened that can be prevented by the court.

Answer (C) is incorrect. The practical inability to tear down the building once it is completed makes the injunctive remedy more attractive to the Nimbes. However, that is not a legal reason for qualifying for an injunction.

Answer (D) is incorrect. The zoning code permits the land use of an apartment building, but it does not authorize nuisances or other interferences with the enjoyment of the neighbors' properties. Therefore the zoning code is not an absolute barrier to an injunction. Rather, to get an injunction, the plaintiffs must first show some violation of the law, which is made more difficult by the authorization of the specific land use.

65. **Answer (B) is the correct answer.** Courts consider the public policy or public interest when weighing the factors in favor of an injunction. The policy against forcing an employee to work for an employer, embodied in the Thirteenth Amendment, is a strong legal policy that weighs against the issuance of the injunction in this case. While crafting a negative injunction prohibiting Woo from playing for the Tempo might arguably be less intrusive of her rights, it effectively accomplishes the same result of forcing Woo to remain in Akron by foreclosing the one other employment opportunity available to Woo. Thus, the public policy against forced employment would likely trump to deny the negative injunction.

Answer (A) is incorrect. Woo may be famous, but not necessarily unique, as there are other softball players available to replace her on the team. Even assuming that Woo is unique, due to her famous personality and particular abilities, the public policy against personal servitude outweighs the plaintiff's preference for an injunction in this case.

Answer (C) is incorrect because enforcing the employment contract does not impose substantial undue hardship upon Woo. All defendants have some hardship from imposition of an injunction. It is only significant undue hardship or economic waste, such as the inability of Woo to play or work at all, that would rise to the level sufficient to disqualify the injunction.

Answer (D) is incorrect. The law does enforce written promises, but usually by the remedy of compensatory damages rather than injunction. The general moral policy of enforcing promises alone is insufficient to qualify for an injunction.

66. Betty should seek both damages and an injunction for Sid's violation of her copyright. Damages would provide her with money to replace the loss of the copyright in the past. However, for the future, she should seek injunctive relief in order to prevent any further, continued loss. The injunction would operate *in personam* against Sid and force him to credit her properly with the rights to the song. This would result in any future profits from the song itself being properly awarded to her, thereby avoiding any uncertainty in the measurement of damages based on these future profits.

67. **Answer (D) is the correct answer.** A court will issue a preventive injunction to protect the plaintiff against a real threat of imminent harm. Here, the existence of a dangerous animal in a residential neighborhood poses a real threat of imminent harm and assault.

Answer (A) is incorrect because even though the tiger is the neighbor's property, the neighbor may not lawfully use his property to threaten harm to others.

Answer (B) is incorrect. Although the tiger has not yet caused harm to anyone, the court need not wait until harm occurs before acting. All that is required for an injunction is a real threat, not an actual completed event. Courts prefer to avoid personal injury rather than waiting for the physical harm to occur. While damages could be awarded to the plaintiff, courts prefer as a matter of public policy to protect individuals from physical harm.

Answer (C) is incorrect. The rule of strict liability regarding inherently dangerous objects is irrelevant to the question of whether an injunction should issue. While it might help establish the basis for tort liability, the dangerous nature alone does not justify the issuance of an injunction.

68. **Answer (A) is the correct answer.** An injunction is not automatically awarded. Instead, a plaintiff must first establish irreparable injury demonstrating that damages are inadequate to remedy the harm. Here, the district court's finding of damages from the harm suggests that damages are in fact adequate for the plaintiff. The court's reasoning is thus flawed because it negates, rather than supports, the legal existence of irreparable injury.

Answer (B) is incorrect. The court's reasoning here is not flawed, as the preliminary injunction is not relevant to the request for a permanent injunction. Preliminary relief is sought when there is immediate harm. The failure to seek a court injunction for immediate harm in the short term should not impact the decision of the court as to a post-judgment injunction.

Answer (C) is incorrect. The statement is true that public policy is relevant to a court's decision as to whether to grant an injunction. Here, the public policy is clearly embodied in a constitutional provision which supports the strong policy against patent infringement.

Answer (D) is incorrect because injunctions are generally available for all types of cases, unless specifically excluded by statute. Injunctions are available in patent cases, and thus the court's reasoning is not flawed in assuming the availability of such relief.

69. **Answer (B) is the correct answer.** A preventive injunction seeks to prevent future harm by stopping the current illegality. This preventive measure requires Macrocorp to stop the current illegality, thereby preventing the same legal harm in the future.

    Answer (A) is incorrect. This is a prophylactic provision designed to impose an additional, precautionary measure on Macrocorp of requiring a revised, standardized contract for future transactions.

    Answer (C) is incorrect because it is a structural injunctive measure designed to address the illegality inherent in the structure of the company itself, which is too big and too powerful to act competitively in the market.

    Answer (D) is incorrect because it is a reparative measure that seeks to reverse or repair the past illegality by ordering corrective measures to the existing licensing.

70. **Answer (B) is the correct answer.** Prophylactic injunctions, like prophylactic medicine, require the defendant to take extra steps or safeguards to ensure against the repetition of future harm.

    Answer (A) is incorrect and defines preventive injunctions.

    Answer (C) is incorrect and defines reparative injunctions.

    Answer (D) is incorrect, as prophylactic injunctions are valid types of injunctions that can be issued by the courts.

71. The court's order to "stop blocking and assaulting" is a preventive measure that is designed to stop the ongoing harm in the future. The second court order imposing a 35-foot buffer zone around the lab is a prophylactic measure that establishes additional safeguards to address one facilitator of the continued assaults, which is the close physical proximity between the lab and the protestors. This answer of preventive and prophylactic measures is contained in **Answer (C), making (C) the correct answer. Thus, answers (A), (B), and (D) are incorrect.**

72. As Smith's counsel in the sexual harassment suit, you could seek a variety of injunctive measures to return Smith to her rightful position and to prevent similar harm in the future. Preventive measures to stop the harm would order Grant to cease the sexual harassment. Reparative measures of equitable relief would reverse the continuing consequences of the harm, and in this case, might transfer Smith to work for another attorney. The firm could also be ordered to comply with prophylactic measures that would provide additional safeguards to address the facilitators of the harm. For

example, the firm could be ordered to draft a sexual harassment policy, establish a confidential employee grievance procedure, and train managers how to properly handle complaints of harassment.

73. **Answer (D) is the correct answer.** The illegality is the exclusion of men from CHICK, and thus the appropriate injunctive measure that will stop that continued exclusion and restore the individual male plaintiffs to their rightful position is to order access of the men to CHICK. As in the U.S. Supreme Court's decision in the case of *United States v. Virginia*, 518 U.S. 515 (1996) (*VMI*), the state could not evade the requirements of rectifying the ongoing harm by providing a parallel but separate educational opportunity.

     Answer (A) is incorrect because it does not rectify the precise harm found by the court of unconstitutional exclusion. However, this was the relief originally ordered by the court of appeals in the *VMI* case, and the relief that one Supreme Court Justice found to be appropriate.

     Answer (B) is incorrect because it is overbroad in that it reaches beyond the harm of excluding male students to eliminating the entire school.

     Answer (C) is incorrect because it, like answer (B), is overbroad as it reaches beyond the exclusionary harm of the gender discrimination in the admissions policy. In addition, this measure imposes structural relief in the form of privatizing the school, but such structural relief may not issue until the court has given the defendants a first opportunity to remedy the harm. Again, in the real VMI case, this was the option sough to be achieved voluntarily by the school alumni, as a private college would not be a state actor and thus would not be subject to the Equal Protection Clause.

74. The term "structural" injunction was first used in the 1970s to describe injunctions issued by courts in public law cases involving prisons, schools, and mental institutions. These injunctions seemed to differ from common forms of injunctive relief in their scope and in the detail by which they governed many aspects of the day to day functioning of the defendant public institutions. There are three main arguments against structural injunctions. First, it is asserted that judges are engaging in policymaking by inserting their own subjective views of how public institutions should be run. For example, when a judge orders a school to be desegregated, he is merely imposing his own personal view of justice. The second argument against structural injunctions is that they violate principles of federalism, because it is usually federal courts dictating to state agencies how to manage their institutions. Finally, the third argument against structural injunctions is that, in issuing this relief, courts invade the separation of powers with executive and legislative branches by overreaching their realm of control by dictating the daily management of governmental functions.

75. **Answer (C) is the correct answer.** The structural injunction here is invalid because it is too broad in scope because it reaches a myriad of aspects of the prison law library that are unrelated to and disconnected from the legal harm of one illiterate inmate being

denied access to the court. *See Lewis v. Casey*, 518 U.S. 343 (1996) (holding of a unanimous Court).

Answer (A) is incorrect. This is a correct statement of the legal rule that the scope of injunctive relief must match the scope of the harm. However, the application of the rule to the facts shows that the injunction here is too broad in scope because it orders relief unconnected to the proven harm.

Answer (B) is incorrect. As prospective relief, all injunctions must be necessary to prevent future harm. However, the terms of the injunction here go beyond addressing the harm and thus are not necessary to preventing future denials of rights to the inmate harmed or prisoners like him.

Answer (D) is incorrect. Terms of injunctive relief do not need to be constitutionally required where they are prophylactic relief designed to remedy or prevent harm that is constitutionally protected. Prophylactic injunctions provide additional safeguards to address the facilitators of harm, where the prophylactic terms are causally connected to the underlying harm. Here, it is not the content of the injunctive terms that makes the relief invalid, but rather their lack of a nexus to the underlying harm.

76. **Answer (D) is the correct answer.** Specific performance, or an injunction ordering the seller to perform the contract, is available here because Spice's flavorings are unique. The UCC provides that specific performance is available as a remedy for the breach of a contract for the sale of goods where the goods are unique. The uniqueness of the goods is established here by the buyer's inability to find similar flavorings on the market and the distinctiveness of the combination of flavorings.

Answer (A) is incorrect because it denies the injunction and awards incidental damages in the amount of reliance. While incidental damages caused by the defendant's breach are available under the UCC for breaches of contracts for the sale of goods, specific performance would be available here due to the uniqueness of the flavorings which cannot be replaced on the market.

Answer (B) is incorrect because specific performance is available to Cola, and future lost profits as a measure of consequential damages flowing from the breach of contract are likely speculative and unforeseeable and thus not recoverable.

Answer (C) is incorrect because it awards duplicative remedies for Cola's future losses. A plaintiff cannot receive double remedies for the same loss. Here, the answer awards an injunction to avoid future loss but then also awards money in the amount of future lost profits.

77. **Answer (A) is the correct answer.** A defendant may seek modification of an injunction, which is a continuing, prospective remedy, when there are significant changed circumstances of fact or law. Here, the changed factual circumstances of Father's lack of income provide a basis for him to seek modification.

Answer (B) is incorrect because the standard for terminating an injunction is not changed circumstances, but rather requires a good faith compliance with a substantial portion of the injunction.

Answer (C) is incorrect because it mixes the standard for termination (substantial, good faith performance) with the process of modification.

Answer (D) is incorrect. While the answer states the correct standard for termination of an injunction, Father cannot show substantial performance with the order, as he has not supported his daughter for the majority of her childhood. "Substantial" performance is a high standard that does not provide a mechanism for defendants to evade court-ordered obligations.

78. **Answer (C) is the correct answer.** Rocky may seek an injunction against the court to prevent it from requiring the counseling treatment. Mandamus is a more specific type of injunctive relief, defined as an injunction issued against a judicial or public official directing the official to perform some act which the law obligates the official to perform. Thus, Rocky may also seek the more specific common-law injunctive remedy of mandamus against the court. Declaratory relief also would be appropriate if Rocky wanted to obtain a judicial declaration that the counseling treatment was unconstitutional. The strategic advantage of the declaratory judgment would be that it would not order the sentencing judge to engage in specific conduct, as would an injunction, and thus might avoid any perceived animosity from the judge.

Answers (B) and (D) are incorrect because they include contempt as a possible option for Rocky. Contempt is not available here because it is an ancillary remedy used to enforce a pre-existing order with which the defendant has failed to comply. Here, there is no prior injunction against the court which the sentencing judge has failed to follow. While Rocky himself might be held in contempt for failing to complete the counseling program as ordered, he cannot obtain the remedy against the judge in the absence of a previous order directing the judge's behavior.

Answer (A) is incorrect because it is incomplete. Rocky may seek an injunction, but he may also request mandamus and declaratory relief. Thus, (C) is the better, more complete answer.

79. Shoe Co. can seek a temporary injunction for the imminent threat of harm to its trademark threatened in the next few days. Shoe Co. can also seek a preliminary injunction that would enjoin the sale of the shoes by Footwork during the litigation. Shoe Co. cannot seek a permanent injunction at this stage of the litigation and must wait until a final determination on the merits at the completion of trial. Thus, Shoe Co. can seek both a temporary and preliminary injunction which is contained in **Answer (B), making it the correct answer. Answers (A), (C), and (D) are therefore incorrect.**

80. An "*ex parte*" or one-sided order is issued by the court in the presence of only one party. Generally, a party may obtain a temporary restraining order *ex parte* only if it has attempted to provide notice to the adverse party. Most domestic violence laws establish an automatic process that requires no notice to the defendant prior to the issuance of the initial temporary order. Defendants in domestic violence cases have challenged the routine practice of issuing *ex parte* restraining orders on grounds of federal due process. They claim that they have been denied due process by the arbitrary denial of their rights without sufficient notice or process. States have justified such routine denial of due process on the emergency needs of plaintiffs in domestic violence situations and the need to expedite such matters. In addition, the argument is that any due process violation is minimal since the *ex parte* order lasts only about ten days and the defendant is required to have notice of the subsequent hearing for a permanent protective order.

81. **Answer (D) is the correct answer.** Plaintiffs will be able to establish irreparable injury during the operative time period of the preliminary injunction. Between now and the time a trial finally resolves the case, the teachers, students, and parents will have their constitutional rights violated in the form of an intangible right that is difficult to measure. In addition, once the school year begins, the court would not be able to stop the voucher programs without undue hardship to the students who would be required to switch schools in the middle of the school year. Thus, a court would act to enforce the status quo to prevent the irreparable harm to the plaintiff during the litigation.

Answer (A) is incorrect because the balance of hardships between the parties is close. The balance does not weigh significantly in the state's favor towards moving forward with the program nor will the delay impose additional costs on the defendants.

Answer (B) is incorrect because the injunction would further the public interest by advancing the constitutional rights of the parents, teachers, and students in the community. This public interest in favor of the injunction is also mitigated by the public interest against the injunction for those favoring vouchers as a means to provide alternative schooling to children. The public interest factor that weighs both for and against the injunction thus is not determinative of the court's final action.

Answer (C) is incorrect because the likelihood of success on the merits is not determinative here. Plaintiffs can establish a likelihood of success based upon the U.S. Supreme Court case that is binding precedent. However, given the split in authority between the old U.S. Supreme Court case and the newer state Supreme Court case, it is clear that the issue in the case is a close legal question as to the merits of the voucher system that will need to be resolved through full litigation.

82. **Answer (B) is the correct answer.** Federal Rule of Civil Procedure 65(b) requires only that efforts be made to notify the defendant when a request for temporary relief is made. The rule states that a TRO may be granted without written or oral notice to the adverse party only if (1) there is immediate and irreparable injury before the party can be heard in opposition, and (2) the applicant's attorney certifies to the court in writing the efforts, if any, which have been made to give the notice and the reasons supporting his claim.

Answer (A) is incorrect because Federal Rule of Civil Procedure 65 does not require actual or constructive notice to the defendant. The rule permits a TRO to issue without notice to the adverse party if efforts have been made to contact the party.

Answer (C) is incorrect. There is an imminent threat of harm from Fly's suspension in the upcoming championship games that cannot be rectified with money at the conclusion of a full trial.

Answer (D) is incorrect. At the temporary injunction stage, a plaintiff does not have to conclusively prove that there has been a violation of the law. Rather, he must establish that a likely violation of law is threatened. Fly has satisfied that standard here as the denial of a hearing to a student prior to suspension has been held to be a violation of due process.

83. Sabrina may obtain a preliminary injunction to enjoin Sleaze from violating her privacy while the litigation is pending. She has filed her complaint and can show an irreparable harm from Sleaze's continued invasions of her privacy. Sabrina will not be able to obtain temporary relief because there is no threat of imminent harm shown. While Sleaze has violated her rights in the past, he has not committed any violation in the past few weeks, nor are there any facts showing a particularized threat in the upcoming week. Temporary relief only enjoins harm that is threatened before the time the adverse party can be heard in opposition at a hearing. In the absence of that type of threatened harm here, Sabrina cannot obtain a TRO. At this initial stage of the litigation, Sabrina will be unable to obtain a permanent injunction as permanent relief is not available until the conclusion of trial. Thus, Sabrina can obtain only preliminary relief, making **Answer (C) the correct answer. Answers (A), (B), and (D) are incorrect** because they include injunctive relief that is not available to Sabrina.

84. **Answer (B) is the correct answer.** Federal Rule of Civil Procedure 65, as interpreted by the Supreme Court, requires that a party requesting temporary relief make efforts to notify the adverse party of the request for temporary relief. When such efforts are unsuccessful, the rule does allow the court to issue a TRO *ex parte* if the reasons for the lack of notice are explained.

Answer (A) is incorrect. The protestors do pose an immediate threat of harm given their past violent behavior towards people and property and their scheduled continuation of the protest.

Answer (C) is incorrect. While actual notice to the defendant is not absolutely required for a temporary injunction, efforts to notify the defendant must be made. If that notice is ineffective, then the moving party must explain to the court why the temporary injunction can issue despite the lack of notice.

Answer (D) is incorrect. It is true that *ex parte* injunctions where only one party appears before the judge are authorized by law. However, a moving party must qualify for such relief by making efforts to notify the defendant and by demonstrating immediate and irreparable harm. The failure to attempt notice here disqualifies the police from seeking temporary relief.

85. The court will issue a preliminary injunction when: (1) the likelihood of success on the merits favors plaintiff; (2) the plaintiff shows irreparable injury during the pendency of trial; (3) the balance of the hardships between the parties weighs in favor of the plaintiff; and (4) the granting of the injunction advances the public interest.

86. **Answer (D) is the correct answer** because the three types of injunctions differ in all of these characteristics. The three differ in duration in that temporary injunctions last for up to ten days, preliminary injunctions last for the duration of litigation, and permanent injunctions run from the completion of trial until a time designated by the court. The three injunctions also differ in eligibility criteria: TROs require immediate threat of imminent harm and notice efforts to the defendant; PIs require (1) a likelihood of success on the merits, (2) irreparable injury during the trial, (3) balance of hardships in the plaintiff's favor, and (4) furtherance of the public interest; and permanent injunctions require necessity, irreparable injury, no undue burden on the defendant or court, and furtherance of the public interest. Finally, the three differ in time of imposition as TROs are imposed immediately upon request, PIs are imposed at the start of litigation, and permanent injunctions are imposed at the completion of trial. Thus, **Answers (A), (B), and (C) are incorrect** because they are incomplete answers.

87. **Answer (C) is the correct answer.** The black letter law states that the basic goal of a preliminary injunction is to preserve the status quo while the parties litigate the case. Determining the status quo is sometimes difficult when a party, like Charlie, has changed his behavior just prior to the initiation of the lawsuit. Courts thus look for the last uncontested or agreed upon status quo. Here, that last uncontested position would

be Charlie selling snacks at the First and Main location where he worked for over four years without university complaint.

Answer (A) is incorrect because it is overbroad in going beyond the scope of the alleged illegality of selling in the licensed library area. In addition, this injunction alters the status quo prior to the completion of litigation conclusively determining the legal rights of the parties.

Answer (B) is incorrect. Charlie selling snacks at the library is the current status of the parties. However, that status was contested from the time Charlie first relocated. Courts do not permit defendants to create a status quo in their own favor by adopting the allegedly illegal action in a preliminary injunction. Instead, the court will look to the last uncontested status quo between the parties.

Answer (D) is incorrect. The public interest is not strongly implicated in this disagreement between two private parties, and thus would not dictate the ultimate outcome of the request for injunctive relief.

88. Federal Rule of Civil Procedure 65(c) requires that a plaintiff post an injunction bond prior to obtaining temporary or preliminary relief. Many states have similar rules mandating injunction bonds for provisional relief. While the rule appears to mandate injunction bonds in all cases of temporary or preliminary relief, some courts have waived the bond or required only a nominal sum where the applicant does not have an ability to pay or where the suit involves the public interest. The bond requirement provides a secure source of funds from which the defendant can collect damages in case it has been wrongfully enjoined. In some jurisdictions, the amount of the injunction bond caps the amount of damages available to the wrongfully enjoined defendant.

89. **Answer (D) is the correct answer** because the defendant has willfully violated a specific order of the court.

    Answer (A) is incorrect because contempt requires willful, intentional conduct, which is not established here by the accidental underpayment of money.

    Answer (C) is incorrect because the company is under no court order to adopt such polices.

    Answer (B) is incorrect because, while the company is under an obligation generally to produce all relevant documents, in the absence of a specific court directive to produce the identified document, it is unlikely that a court would find the requisite willful intent necessary to establish a contempt violation.

90. **Answer (D) is correct and the best answer** because the vague terms that led to the dispute should be clarified for further judicial efficiency and to guide the parties' respective behavior.

    Answer (A) is incorrect because consent decrees, which are private settlements endorsed by the court as judicial orders, can be enforced by the contempt power. In contrast, private contractual settlements not adopted by the court as its order cannot be enforced with contempt.

    Answer (B) is incorrect because the government's motion is not frivolous, since reasonable minds could differ as to the operational commands of the vague injunctive terms.

    Answer (C) is incorrect because it is an incomplete answer, since the court must do more than simply deny the motion.

91. **Answer (C) is the correct answer.** This is civil coercive contempt because the defendant literally holds the keys to her own cell. She is able to purge the contempt remedy and avoid any consequence by complying with the court's order.

    Answer (A) is incorrect. Summary contempt is immediate punishment for a threat to the court's authority.

    Answer (B) is incorrect. Criminal contempt is to punish the defendant for a past violation of an order with a fixed, determinate sentence. Here, McDonagal's sentence is indeterminate and designed to force future compliance.

Answer (D) is incorrect. Civil compensatory contempt is the imposition of a monetary fine for past harm caused.

92.   Procedural safeguards are required prior to the judicial imposition of a valid contempt remedy. Civil contempt requires notice and an opportunity to be heard. Criminal contempt requires the full range of criminal procedures such as the right to counsel, right to jury, right against self-incrimination, and proof beyond a reasonable doubt. Due process requires these procedures because of potential arbitrariness of a judge who is enforcing her own order against a violator. There is concern that a judge might be overly punitive simply because it is her own command, rather than that of the legislature or another judge, that has been disobeyed. In addition, the procedural safeguards address the potential abuse of power inherent in contempt where the traditional separation of powers is omitted and the judge embodies lawmaker, decisionmaker, and executioner in one.

93.   **Answer (B) is the correct answer.** If Husband refuses to pay the back support by the stated time, he will be ordered to jail without the ability to avoid or purge the contempt. This fixed penalty that punishes Husband for his past failure is criminal contempt that cannot be awarded without a full criminal trial in which all the criminal procedural protections are provided.

       Answer (A) is incorrect because, while contempt does require a willful or intentional violation of a court order, the Husband's refusal to pay in light of his ability to pay is sufficient to establish the required level of intentional violation.

       Answer (C) is incorrect because, while the $4000 is measured based on the amount of plaintiff's loss as appropriate for civil compensatory contempt, the conditioning of that payment and the imposition of an additional punishment creates a hybrid contempt remedy of compensatory and criminal contempt that is not supported with the necessary criminal procedures. If the court awarded only the first part of the remedy, plus measured any other loss to the Wife such as interest lost on the money or the costs of the contempt motion, then it would constitute a valid civil compensatory fine.

       Answer (D) is incorrect because upon day 31, the Husband does not have the ability to purge the contempt remedy and it becomes a fine for past behavior and thus is criminal contempt. The legal problem arises when the judge creates a hybrid contempt remedy, such as this one, that mixes characteristics of criminal and civil remedies thus threatening the legitimacy of the contempt remedy.

94.   Defendants can first challenge the validity of the injunction, arguing that the language was vague and imprecise, giving improper notice of expected conduct. They can establish that there was not a willful violation, but an inability to comply. Alternatively, they can seek a modification of the injunction to better fit the actual circumstances that the defendants find themselves in. Or defendants can seek to terminate the injunction based upon their good faith and substantial compliance over time.

95. **Answer (A) is the correct answer** because the court's power of summary contempt allows the judge to take measures to control the courtroom without further procedures.

    Answer (C) is incorrect because the procedures for civil contempt are not required when the authority of the court is directly threatened.

    Answer (B) is incorrect because it is an incomplete statement of procedures that would be required in a civil contempt context, and because the ability to issue summary contempt here negates the requirement of any further proceedings.

    Answer (D) is incorrect because the act of jailing the defendant does not make the contempt criminal in nature. Jail time is a proper consequence of summary, civil, and criminal contempt.

96. **Answer (B) is the correct answer** because the court attempted two criminal contempt fines to punish the defendants for past contumacious acts. The assessment of a per assault fine when imposed upon defendants after the occurrence of the act becomes fixed and unavoidable and thus constitutes criminal contempt. Just as in the lead U.S. Supreme Court case of *Int'l Mine Workers v. Bagwell*, 512 U.S. 821 (1994), the Court's prior announcement of the remedy does not save the contempt from being a fixed penalty for past behavior. However, the lack of adequate criminal procedural safeguards, discussed in **Answer A**, renders this criminal contempt invalid.

    Answer (A) is incorrect because the criminal contempt orders of the court are invalid because the court did not adopt the full panoply of criminal safeguards required, instead using only one isolated criminal safeguard of the burden beyond a reasonable doubt. The hybrid civil/criminal hearing is insufficient procedural protection prior to the imposition of criminal contempt.

    Answer (C) is incorrect because the advanced announcement of the fines does not make them avoidable. If the defendants commit ten assaults, they will be required to pay a fixed fine of $100,000 with no ability to purge. A civil coercive remedy must be avoidable at the time of the imposition of the fine so that the defendant may be said to "hold the keys to her own cell." This prior announcement of fines calibrated on a per violation basis was expressly struck down by the U.S. Supreme Court in *Bagwell*.

    Answer (D) is incorrect on the facts given, as the court did in fact conduct the required hearing.

97. **Answer (B) is the correct answer** because compensatory contempt is a monetary fine measured by the amount of loss caused by the defendants' lack of compliance with the court's injunction.

    Answer (A) is incorrect because the fine is not future oriented with the purpose of coercing compliance with the order by fines that are avoidable.

Answer (C) is incorrect because the fines for past conduct here are not fixed, determinate fines, but instead are calibrated to the exact measure of loss caused by the defendant.

Answer (D) is incorrect because, while a monetary remedy measured by plaintiff's loss would be compensatory damages, the remedy here is imposed after a hearing at the end of an ongoing action, rather than in response to a trial in a new action brought against the defendants.

98. **Answer (A) is the correct answer.** A restitution theory of recovery does not apply here because there is no unjust enrichment to the defendant. Builder has not received a profit or gain unjustly at plaintiff's expense. The problem with the non-conforming building and the additional remodeling expenses involves a loss to Joe that is addressed by compensatory damages.

    Answer (B) is incorrect. Irreparable injury is a requirement for injunctive relief. If Joe had suffered irreparable injury, he would be able to seek equitable relief in the form of an injunction or equitable restitution (*i.e.*, constructive trust or equitable lien). However, those remedial options are not what Joe is seeking in this case nor has he established that damages or legal restitution are inadequate to redress his injury.

    Answer (C) is incorrect because if Joe wanted to punish Builder for the loss caused, Joe would seek punitive damages rather than restitution. In addition, punitive damages are not available for breach of contract and require the existence of a tort claim.

    Answer (D) is incorrect. Restitution is not based upon plaintiff's loss, but is focused on defendant's gain. If Joe wants money to compensate for his losses, he would seek compensatory damages.

99. **Answer (C) is the correct answer.** Landlord can sue in quasi-contract to obtain restitution for the Tenant's unauthorized use of the machine. Quasi-contract is a fictional theory that implies a contract at law as a basis for awarding monetary relief.

    Answer (A) is incorrect. Quantum meruit is a restitution theory seeking recovery for the value of a plaintiff's services unjustly conferred upon the defendant. Here, Landlord has not conferred a service upon the Tenant.

    Answer (B) is incorrect. Constructive trust is an equitable restitution theory that implies a fictional trust and holds the defendant accountable as a trustee for the benefits accrued from the wrongdoing. Constructive trust generally requires fraud and the use of the plaintiff's specific property. Here, there is no fraud or breach of trust involved in the dispute, and thus constructive trust would not be an appropriate theory.

    Answer (D) is incorrect. Rescission is a restitution theory that cancels the contract and returns the parties to their original pre-contract positions. Here, there is no actual contract regarding the use of the machine to cancel.

100. All of these measures are potential measurements of relief in restitution cases. The appropriateness of a measure depends upon which measurement best fits the facts and theory of the case and that which disgorges all of the benefit to the culpable defendant.

Here, the operative theory of restitution is quasi-contract and contract measures generally look to an objective market measure of the worth of the item at issue. Thus, the market rental or purchase value of the machine would be a common default measure in this case. The market value of the entire machine best fits the facts of the case as Tenant converted the entire machine for its use. However, because plaintiff elected restitution instead of damages for the tort of conversion, a court would not limit him to a damages-like measure. In addition, the use of a market measure of a ten-year-old depreciated machine would not disgorge the full benefit from the culpable defendant who converted the machine. Thus, **Answers (A) and (B) are incorrect.** A profit measure that disgorges the benefit gained by the defendant from the machine would be more appropriate. The profits would be apportioned to disgorge only that measure of profits associated with the wrong, the **correct answer as indicated in Answer (C).** Thus, the profits made from the design and marketing of the product indicated in **Answer (D) is incorrect** and would not be an appropriate measure.

101.   Quantum meruit is a claim to recover the value of services rendered. It is a more specialized subset of the general claim of quasi-contract which is an implied at law contract for the value of the benefit gained by the defendant. Here, the more specific action of quantum meruit is appropriate for Artista to seek recovery of the value of her design services provided to the University. Thus, **Answers (A) and (B) are incorrect.** Under the majority rule, if she sues for quantum meruit for partial performance of a contract, she is not suing under the contract and thus the value of her services is not measured by the value of the contract ($5000). The objective value of her services can be measured by her actual cost of $9000 worth of actual services rendered. *See Boomer v. Muir,* 24 P.2d 570 (Cal. Ct. App. 1933). This is a situation of a "losing contract," where a party has entered into a contract that, if performed, would lose her money. By virtue of the cancellation of the contract and her partial performance, the plaintiff gains an opportunity to sue in restitution for the value of the services rendered under the theory that the design work was intended for University's benefit. Thus, the **best answer here is Answer (D)** that Artista can sue in quantum meruit for the $9000 and **Answer (C) is incorrect.** It should be noted that a few jurisdictions would limit Artista's recovery to the value of the contract ($5000) to preclude any windfall above the contract expectancy. A few other jurisdictions would measure her services by the contract value of $5000 and limit her to recovery of 90% ($4500) of that for her partial performance.

102.   **Answer (B) is the correct answer.** In order for a unilateral mistake to be the basis for rescission, that mistake must be known or should have been known to the other side. Here, the mathematical error was Bionicle's unilateral mistake, but it was not known to Lego. Furthermore, the fact that Bionicle's bid was $25,000 lower than the other bids of $200,000 is insufficient to establish that Lego should have known of the mistake.

   Answer (A) is incorrect because the fact that the mistake was made before the time of the bid is irrelevant to the availability of rescission.

Answer (C) is incorrect because the facts do not establish the existence of a bilateral mistake since Lego was not aware of a mistake.

Answer (D) is incorrect because a unilateral mistake, alone, is not sufficient to qualify for rescission. The mistake must be known (or should have been known) to the other side.

103. **Answer (C) is the correct answer.** Unjust enrichment of the defendant is not established when the plaintiff volunteers the benefit. Here, Accountant volunteered his services, and thus the defendant's benefit was not unjustly obtained at the plaintiff's expense.

Answer (A) is incorrect. The answer describes a recovery in quantum meruit for the value of the services provided by Accountant. However, the predicate basis of unjust enrichment is not established where the accountant has volunteered the services.

Answer (B) is incorrect. Restitution is unavailable as indicated in **Answers A and C** because Accountant volunteered the services. In addition, this answer provides a measure of plaintiff's loss, which is a measure of compensatory damages rather than a measure of defendant's benefit.

Answer (D) is incorrect because the neighbor did in fact receive a benefit in the form of the tax preparation services provided by Accountant.

104. **Answer (B) is the correct answer.** The doctrine of promissory estoppel provides that a promise reasonably expected to induce action and that does induce detrimental reliance is an enforceable promise limited to recovery of reliance damages. The promise by Almondia of "don't worry, we'll work things out" is a promise reasonably expected to induce action that did induce detrimental reliance in the extra costs incurred by Distributor.

Answer (A) is incorrect. There is no implied-in-fact contract because the facts and circumstances here do not establish the existence of an actual contract upon which to base recovery. There was never a meeting of the minds as to the terms of the distributorship agreement.

Answer (C) is incorrect. Unjust enrichment arises if there is a benefit to defendant. Here, there was no benefit resulting to Almondia from Distributors' additional workers and larger lease space.

Answer (D) is incorrect. Quasi-contract is a restitution remedy when there is an unjust benefit retained by the defendant. As described in **Answer (C),** no benefit accrued to Almondia here. However, in a few jurisdictions where promissory estoppel is not available, some courts might apply quasi-contract to address the inequity of plaintiff's performance done with the intention to benefit the defendant.

105. The restitution remedies of subrogation, indemnity, and contribution may all be involved in this case. These three restitution remedies are implicated by the involvement of three or more parties in the underlying dispute. The basis for restitution in all of these

is the theory that one party has been unjustly enriched when its debt has been unfairly paid by another. Subrogation may be sought by Driver's insurance company to seek reimbursement for the medical expenses paid from any monetary damages Driver might receive from the second negligent driver in the accident litigation. Driver might seek indemnification from its employer due to the Restaurant's promise to cover any legal problems related to the delivery policy. Indemnification provides for reimbursement when one person pays for the debt or liability of another. Indemnity here would mean that Restaurant would pay for any monies Driver would be ordered to pay in the underlying accident suit. Finally, contribution might be an applicable remedy between Driver and the second driver who were both liable in the underlying accident. Contribution is an action between two liable parties when one party has paid more than his fair share of the obligation.

106. **Answer (D) is the correct answer.** The fraud of the CEO creates a basis to rescind the contract. In addition, the unilateral mistake known to the CEO (that Insurance Co. mistakenly believed it was insuring a non-smoker) is an alternative basis upon which to seek rescission. Rescission then restores both parties to their pre-contract position. Thus, the insurance contract is cancelled, no payout is due, and Big Corporation is entitled to the return of the premiums it paid over the several months.

Answer (A) is incorrect. Rescission is appropriate here due to the fraud of the CEO. However, both parties and not just Insurance Co. must be returned to their pre-contract position.

Answer (B) is incorrect. Insurance Co. would be successful in its claim for restitution due to the fraud of the CEO, or alternatively due to the unilateral mistake that it was insuring a non-smoker that was known to the CEO on the other side of the bargain.

Answer (C) is incorrect. This would be a proper measure of compensatory damages if Insurance Co. sued under the contract for its losses from the CEO's breach. However, the facts indicate that Insurance Co. is suing here in restitution, which is a more attractive remedy as it saves the company $3 million rather than accruing a few hundred dollars more in premiums due.

107. **Answer (D) is correct.** The facts of the check and its deposit into the bank account provide circumstantial evidence to establish that an actual contract was created between the parties. An implied-in-fact contract is not a restitution theory, but rather a theory to establish a contractual basis upon which to seek further legal or equitable relief.

Answer (A) is incorrect. To rescind a contract, there must be fraud, duress, substantial breach of contract, mutual mistake of fact, or unilateral mistake known to the other side. While the substantial breach of contract would provide a basis to seek rescission here, the end result desired by Public Agency — the delivery of the computer screens — could not be obtained by rescission. Rescission would cancel the contract and restore the $20,000 payment to Public Agency.

Answer (B) is incorrect. The facts indicate that there is no express contract proven by the evidence at trial either by evidence of a written agreement or evidence of an offer and acceptance.

Answer (C) is incorrect. Quasi-contract is an implied-in-law contract, a fictional analogy, used as a vehicle to award a remedy in the absence of any contractual or other legal basis for liability. This implication is not necessary here where the facts establish the existence of an actual contract upon which Public Agency can sue.

108. **Answer (A) is the correct answer.** Quasi-contract is a legal restitution theory that is a contract implied at law to disgorge the defendant's unjust gain.

   Answer (B) is incorrect. A constructive trust is an equitable restitution claim that implies a fictionalized trust to disgorge the profit retained by the defendant at the plaintiff's expense.

   Answer (C) is incorrect. An equitable lien is an equitable restitution remedy that secures a debt owed to the plaintiff with the defendant's tangible property.

   Answer (D) is incorrect. An accounting of profits is an equitable restitution remedy that requires the defendant to account for and then disgorge the amount of profit unjustly gained by the defendant at the plaintiff's expense.

109. The hallmarks of equitable restitution are its historical origins, its tracing capacity, the possibility of an irreparable injury requirement, and the unavailability of a jury trial. It should be noted, however, that there is much inconsistency in the law with respect to the application of these rules. Equitable restitution includes those forms of restitution that historically developed in the courts of chancery. In England, restitution developed as specific writs in both courts of law and equity to address gaps in relief provided by other causes of action. The historical equitable restitution claims are constructive trust, equitable lien, and accounting of profits. Like other equitable remedies, equitable restitution does not include the right to a jury trial and may trigger the irreparable injury rule requiring that legal remedies are inadequate. Equitable relief also permits the plaintiff to "trace" the funds by following the money through changes in forms and ownership. This tracing enhances the valuation of the benefit and the ability to collect the funds through bankruptcy and other creditor situations.

110. **Answer (C) is the correct answer.** The general measure of restitution under a constructive trust remedy is the amount of profits and appreciation of those profits retained by the defendant. Here, the parents have benefited from the addition of a house to their farm land which caused an appreciation in value of $200,000 ($220,000 current value minus $20,000 original value of farm land). Winifred's marital share (50% as Winifred and Harry split marital property equally) of that appreciation is $100,000.

   Answer (A) is incorrect. The $22,000 is the value of Winifred's services put into the house and thus is a measure of quantum meruit.

   Answer (B) is incorrect. The $85,000 represents Winifred's marital share of the financial investment in the home and would constitute a partial measurement of the debt owed to her under an equitable lien theory. However, it does not represent a measure of the profit gained by the parents.

Answer (D) is incorrect. The $107,000 represents the total of Winifred's financial and in-kind investments into the home, as indicated in the **Answer to Question 111**, below. This is an appropriate amount under an equitable lien theory which measures the amount of debt owed to the plaintiff from the benefit unjustly retained by the defendant.

111.   **Answer (D) is the correct answer.** An equitable lien is measured by the amount of debt owed to the plaintiff from the unjust benefit gained by the defendant. Here, the defendant parents unjustly gained from Winifred's financial assistance (1/2 of $30,000 + $140,000 = $85,000) and construction services ($22,000) related to the house that total $107,000.

Answer (A) is incorrect. The $22,000 is the value of Winifred's services put into the house and thus is a measure of quantum meruit.

Answer (B) is incorrect. The $85,000 represents Winifred's marital share of the financial investment in the home, but constitutes only a partial measurement of the debt owed to her under an equitable lien theory.

Answer (C) is incorrect. The $100,000 represents Winifred's marital share of the total appreciation of the house gained by the parents. This measure of profit and appreciation is appropriately awarded under a constructive trust theory, as indicated in the **Answer to Question 110 above.**

112.   **Answer (C) is the correct answer.** A constructive trust would disgorge all of the profits from Bonnie's fraudulent use of her mother-in-law's recipes. Constructive trust is available when the plaintiff originally owned the property at issue and when the defendant commits a wrong involving fraud or breach of a confidence. Both of these elements are satisfied in this scenario.

Answer (A) is incorrect. An equitable lien is a restitution remedy used to secure a debt owed to plaintiff with the tangible property of the defendant at issue. Here, the mother-in-law is not seeking repayment of a debt, but rather seeking to disgorge Bonnie's unjust gain.

Answer (B) is incorrect. Quasi-contract would imply a contract at law between the two women for Bonnie to use her mother-in-law's recipes in the book. The measure of the rental or purchase value of those recipes would not be the amount of Bonnie's total profits.

Answer (D) is incorrect. An accounting of profits remedy would disgorge the benefits unjustly gained by Bonnie at the expense of her mother-in-law, but allow her to retain any profit she derived from her own efforts. The facts here do not indicate that any of the profits were related to Bonnie's own efforts, and thus this remedial option is not appropriate.

113. **Answer (C) is the correct answer.** Bob would use an equitable lien theory to recover the debt owed to him for his improvements to Gretta's house in the amount of the money he loaned to her for the construction on the house.

     Answer (A) is incorrect. Quantum meruit would allow Bob to recover the value of services provided. However, Bob did not provide any construction or remodeling services in this case.

     Answer (B) is incorrect. A constructive trust remedy would be attractive to Bob in order to recover the appreciated value of the house ($70,000) due to his remodeling work. However, constructive trust is not available to Bob because Bob does not have a claim to ownership of the house or a severable interest in the house. Constructive trust requires the plaintiff to have a claim to ownership of the property over which the constructive trust will be imposed. Additionally, constructive trust generally requires a fraud-like wrong on the part of the defendant, and Gretta did nothing to defraud or breach a confidence with Bob.

     Answer (D) is incorrect. Indemnification is available only when there is an agreement between the parties that one party will assume liability if the second is found liable to a third party. No such third party liability is at issue here.

114. The slavery reparations cases seek restitution in the form of monetary payments for the uncompensated labor of the slaves. A constructive trust theory has been used, arguing that the slave owners, and companies like banks and insurance companies that financed slavery, unjustly benefited from the labor of the slaves and held that profit in trust for the slave beneficiaries. A theory of equitable lien also works to seek monetary relief for the slaves' work to improve the value of other people's land. Where strict doctrinal rules of constructive trust fail, because the jurisdiction requires that the plaintiff demonstrate prior ownership of the property, equitable lien assists the slaves in seeking payment for the debt owned by the slave owners of the benefit conferred upon the farming and working of the owners' land. Plaintiffs have also used the legal restitution theories of quasi-contract and quantum meruit to obtain the value of the labor services provided by the slaves.

115. **Answer (C) is the correct answer.** Under an accounting of profits, a plaintiff is awarded only those profits attributed to the wrongful conduct. The plaintiff has the burden of proving the total amount of revenues, and the defendant has the burden of proving its costs and any profits generated from its own efforts rather than the wrong. Here, the $3 million in total revenues was offset by the $2 million in costs, and then further reduced by the $250,000 in profits attributed to the defendant's own lawful advertising actions, leaving $750,000 as the restitution measure of recovery.

     Answer (A) is incorrect. Three million is the total amount of revenues earned by the defendant during the time of the wrong. It could be the measure of recovery under different facts if the defendant failed to prove any offsetting costs or lawful profits. The shared burden of the accounting for profits remedy gives this advantage to the plaintiff in not having to prove the precise amount of offsetting benefits, as this information is usually in the possession of the defendant.

Answer (B) is incorrect. One million is the amount of total profits ($3 million) offset by the defendant's costs of production ($2 million). It fails to take into account the profits earned by the lawful advertising conduct of the defendant ($250,000), which should not be awarded to the defendant.

Answer (D) is incorrect. The amount of Beerman's lost profits proven at trial was $0. However, the amount of plaintiff's loss is a compensatory measure, whereas restitution measures the amount of defendant's gain. The difference is important in cases like this one involving trademark infringement, where it is difficult to prove the losses to plaintiff, or where the defendant gains more than the plaintiff loses.

116.   **Answer (B) is the correct answer.** Equitable restitution uses the tracing device to follow a plaintiff's funds through changes in form and ownership in order to restore the unjust gain to the plaintiff. Tracing thus allows the church to reach the funds in possession of a third party, because Betty is not a bona fide purchaser for value. Here, the original $200,000 of embezzled funds can be traced to the $100,000 cash given to Betty — the $50,000 purchase of the car now worth $30,000 — and the $50,000 in stocks now worth $100,000.

Answer (A) is incorrect. Tracing follows the funds through the changes in form, including appreciation and depreciation of the original amounts. Here, the original $100,000 given to Betty can be traced to a change in value of the appreciated stocks and the depreciated car.

Answer (C) is incorrect. The amount of $150,000 would give the church the appreciated amount of the stocks ($100,000), but not properly trace the car to its current depreciated value.

Answer (D) is incorrect. Of the original amount embezzled ($200,000), only $100,000 can be traced to Betty from LeMar's gift. Betty is not responsible for the total original amount embezzled that cannot be traced to her.

117.   **Answer (B) is the correct answer.** An equitable lien will be awarded and secured by tangible property for the value of a debt owed by another for benefits unjustly conferred and secured by tangible property. Here, Jane owes a debt to Dick for his addition to her home measured by his financial investment and construction services. The security mechanism of the equitable lien allows Dick to foreclose on Jane's house if she does not pay him the amount owed.

Answer (A) is incorrect. The value of Dick's services is an incomplete measure of the debt owed to Dick because it does not include the financial investment of $10,000 that he made in Jane's property.

Answer (C) is incorrect. A constructive trust is measured by the amount of profits earned by the defendant and any appreciation (or depreciation). Jane received more benefit than the $10,000 in savings from the addition to her home and its appreciation ($140,000), though part of that appreciation is due to market forces.

Answer (D) is incorrect. Dick will not be awarded a constructive trust in many jurisdictions because he does not have a claim to ownership of the home. Instead, courts will use an equitable lien as a restitution device to address the improvements made by a party to the property of another. The equitable lien measures the defendant's benefit by the amount of debt owed and not by the amount of profit obtained by the defendant. Thus, the appreciation of the house owned by Jane will not be awarded to Dick.

118. **Answer (D) is the correct answer** because the arrest of Laurel's friend for the exact same activity and the police warning of Laurel for continuing to engage in the leafleting demonstrate that the time is right for the court to issue its declaration due to the real and imminent threat against Laurel.

  Answer (A) is incorrect. While the fact that Laurel has stopped the conduct raises a question as to whether the controversy is ripe, there are no further facts or actions that are necessary to complete the controversy short of Laurel leafleting again, which would subject him to the penalty of arrest and jail time. This is exactly what the declaratory judgment seeks to avoid.

  Answer (B) is incorrect because if he wants an order against the police to cease and desist, he should choose an injunctive remedy.

  Answer (C) is incorrect because the dispute between Laurel and the Village is adverse as both sides disagree about the concrete issue of the application of the criminal trespass statute to the definite conduct by Laurel of leafleting in the Village.

119. **Answer (A) is the correct answer.** The controversy is hypothetical, as Howell seeks general advice as to the interpretation of a term in the contract. The adversity of the conflict is also not established by the facts as it is not known whether XYZ employer will disagree with Howell's exclusion of Internet sales from the contract anti-competition clause.

  Answer (B) is incorrect because declaratory judgments are available in contract, such as business or insurance contracts, to avoid harm in advance of a breach.

  Answer (C) is incorrect because the controversy is not ripe. Howell is just wondering about the possibilities under the contract and has not yet taken all steps necessary (such as speaking with the employer, investigating the Internet business, or leaving his current position) to make the dispute imminent and ripe for the court's decision.

  Answer (D) is incorrect because the mandatory requirement of an "actual controversy" is not established here because the dispute is hypothetical, not adverse, and not ripe.

120. **Answer (C) is the correct answer.** The controversy is ripe because all facts are completed to join the issue and there is an imminent threat that the League will violate the antitrust laws by imposing the fine on the team. All facts necessary to the dispute are completed short of requiring the League to take the final step of fining the team, which would then prevent it from avoiding the antitrust penalties of treble damages and attorney fees that the declaration seeks to avoid.

Answer (A) is incorrect because the team's move does not render the dispute unripe. The desired action is the imposition of a fine, not a prohibition of the move.

Answer (B) is incorrect. The controversy is definite and concrete because the League seeks a statement about the specific question of imposing a fine against the Ships for this move, rather than a generalized ruling as to its possible legal actions under the antitrust laws.

Answer (D) is incorrect as it states a rule of law that is irrelevant to qualifying for a declaratory judgment.

121.   A litigant would choose a declaratory judgment remedy as a preventive remedy to avoid a future harm. The declaratory judgment prevents harm similar to an injunction, but is preferable because unlike an injunction, it does not have an irreparable injury requirement and it allows a jury trial. Many civil rules also expedite hearings for cases seeking only a declaratory judgment, and thus a resolution could be obtained more quickly. Declaratory judgments allow litigants to avoid penalties that might be incurred by proceeding with questionable conduct in the absence of a declaration. For example, a protester seeking to pass out leaflets in violation of a criminal law would prefer to seek a declaration that the statute violates her constitutional rights under the First Amendment prior to being arrested and incurring the penalty of jail. In another example, a business seeking to challenge the constitutionality of a tax would prefer to seek a declaration rather than refusing to pay the tax and potentially incurring additional fines for the failure to pay the tax. Finally, litigants might choose a declaratory judgment in order to avoid acrimonious litigation and to preserve ongoing business relations as in the case of long-term contractual agreements.

122.   **Answer (D) is the correct answer** because declaratory judgments provide a mechanism to enforce the prior statement of the court with additional remedies such as restitution, damages, or injunctions when necessary and proper. Here further relief is necessary and proper since the Maniacs have not voluntarily complied with the court's statement as to copyright ownership.

Answer (A) is incorrect because, while it provides the correct definition of what a declaratory judgment is, it incorrectly states that there is no enforcement mechanism for the remedy.

Answer (B) is incorrect because a plaintiff with a prior declaration does not need to begin legal action anew with a separate complaint.

Answer (C) is incorrect because contempt is an enforcement remedy only for injunctions, not declaratory judgments. Declaratory judgments are authoritative statements of the court, but they are not *in personam* orders that mandate compliance by the defendant. It is only injunctive relief that can be enforced by contempt.

123. **Answer (B) is the correct answer.** A declaratory judgment should not issue here because the movant seeks a declaration about a completed event, which is an inappropriate use of the court's discretion, as it is unable to prevent future harm.

Answer (A) is incorrect because a decision as to vicarious liability would terminate the uncertainty of MLB regarding its legal responsibility in this case.

Answer (C) is incorrect because while the case is ripe, there is an additional discretionary reason to deny the declaratory judgment. The case is ripe because all facts necessary to the dispute have been completed. However, the court should use its discretion to deny the declaration since the controversy concerns a completed event and because of MLB's likely misuse of the declaratory remedy to forum shop and preempt the plaintiff's choice of forum.

Answer (D) is incorrect because, while the controversy is adverse in that MLB and Soza likely disagree over MLB's responsibility, there are additional discretionary reasons to deny the declaratory judgment here.

124. The Uniform Declaratory Judgments Act provides in § 1 that the state courts have power to declare "rights, status, or other legal relations" of the parties. Parties may seek a declaration about a contract (UDJA §§ 2 & 3), the administration of a will (§ 4), or any other topic (§ 5). Declaratory judgments are discretionary, and the court may refuse to issue the remedy if it would "not terminate the uncertainty or controversy giving rise to the proceeding" (§ 6). Declaratory judgments are subject to appellate review in the same manner as any other order (§ 7), and issues of fact are tried to the jury (§ 9). Costs associated with declaratory relief may be awarded (§ 10). Supplemental or further relief is available whenever "necessary and proper" (§ 9).

125. **Answer (C) is the correct answer.** The requested declaratory judgment will not terminate the uncertainty as to whether the insurance company must cover the loss or defend the teacher's lawsuit because the declaration addresses only one of three charges against the teacher. Even if molestation were excluded from coverage, the other two charges might fall within the policy's coverage.

Answer (A) is incorrect. There is an actual controversy between the teacher and the insurance company. However, the discretionary standards still weigh against issuance of the declaration even though the mandatory bases for judicial power have been satisfied.

Answer (B) is incorrect because like **Answer (A),** it addresses only the threshold mandatory bases for judicial power, rather than completing the analysis with a determination as to whether the court's discretion is proper.

Answer (D) is incorrect as there is no impermissible tactical advantage sought by the insurance company. It may use declaratory relief to seek a determination about coverage prior to the determination of the insured's loss.

126.   **Answer (B) is the correct answer.** Paul might use unconscionability as a defense based on the procedural unfairness in the creation of the contract. Unconscionability prohibits the enforcement of an oppressive contract when either the terms or the formation of the contract are substantially unfair. Here, the cancellation terms of the contract and the legal representation on only one side suggest unfairness in the formation of the contract.

   Answer (A) is incorrect. *In pari delicto* is a defense that bars a plaintiff's remedy if the plaintiff's own conduct is equally at fault in the unlawful activity at issue in the case. John has not engaged in any wrongdoing related to the alleged breach of contract in running the business inappropriately.

   Answer (C) is incorrect. Unclean hands bars a plaintiff's recovery where the plaintiff has engaged in wrongful conduct. Here, John has not engaged in any misconduct by enforcing the terms of the contract that are favorable to his interests.

   Answer (D) is incorrect. Estoppel bars a plaintiff's recovery where the plaintiff has engaged in inconsistent conduct and changed a prior position upon which the defendant has relied. John did not change his position with respect to whether or not the contract was breached, and thus there is no basis for asserting the defense of estoppel.

127.   *In pari delicto* and unclean hands both relate to a plaintiff's wrongdoing or misconduct. *In pari delicto* is a legal defense meaning "in equal fault." Unclean hands is an equitable defense derived from the legal maxim that "he who comes into equity must come with clean hands." Unclean hands applies to misconduct that is connected with the controversy at issue in the case. *In pari delicto* applies when the plaintiff's misconduct is closely connected with the controversy and is equal to or greater than that of the defendant. Thus, *in pari delicto* is a legal defense requiring plaintiff misconduct contributing to the harm that is equal to or greater than the defendant's misconduct. Unclean hands is an equitable defense that bars relief based on plaintiff's related misconduct that may not be as bad as the defendant's behavior.

128.   **Answer (A) is the correct answer.** The center could use estoppel to bar the landlord's eviction remedy because it detrimentally relied on the landlord's prior inconsistent statement. Estoppel prevents a party from changing positions when the adverse party has relied upon a prior position. Here, the center relied on the landlord's first statement that he "understood the need for the fence" and thus the landlord is prevented from changing that position to say that the fence now constitutes a basis for eviction.

Answer (B) is incorrect. Laches is a remedial defense related to a party's unreasonable delay in the case. Here, the four-week time period prior to the landlord's action is not an unreasonable amount of time to wait before taking legal action based upon the fence.

Answer (C) is incorrect. Unclean hands is a remedial defense based upon the plaintiff's misconduct. The landlord has not engaged in any misconduct. His expressed understanding of the center's need for the fence is not fraudulent or wrongful.

Answer (D) is incorrect. There was no oppression in the process or the substance of the original lease agreement that could form the basis for an unconscionability argument about the substantial unfairness of enforcing the contract.

129. **Answer (C) is the correct answer.** The Neighbor's misconduct of trespass from the roof overhang establishes a bar to Neighbor's request for relief because it relates to the issue of encroachments by a neighbor.

Answer (A) is incorrect. *In pari delicto,* like unclean hands, is based upon the plaintiff's misconduct. However, *in pari delicto* requires that the misconduct have a nexus to the activity at issue in the lawsuit. Here, the Neighbor's misconduct regarding the roof is not directly connected to the legal issue of trespass regarding the pool. Also, it is not clear that Neighbor is more at fault than Homeowner.

Answer (B) is incorrect. Waiver is the relinquishment of a known right. There are no facts to suggest that Neighbor gave up his right to the property or otherwise approved the encroachment of the swimming pool.

Answer (D) is incorrect. Unconscionability is a remedial defense related to the formation of a contract, and there is no contract at issue in the dispute between Neighbor and Homeowner.

130. **Answer (D) is the correct answer.** Doctor could use the remedial defense of laches due to the patient's four-year delay in prosecuting the action that caused prejudice to the doctor. The four-year delay is not excused by the busy trial schedule of the lawyers. The patient's delay in initiating discovery caused the doctor prejudice because evidence and witnesses that might benefit Doctor's defense in the lawsuit are now unavailable.

Answer (A) is incorrect because the statute of limitations sets a specific time for commencing the action and does not address the post-commencement delay. Here, Patient complied with the statute of limitations by filing and serving the complaint within three years of the date of the alleged negligence.

Answer (B) is incorrect because Patient has not engaged in any misconduct or bad acts that would bar relief in the case.

Answer (C) is incorrect because Patient has not waived the right to pursue a remedy by unilaterally relinquishing a known right.

131.   Plaintiff's conduct serves as a bar to recovery because it would be unfair to allow a "bad" plaintiff to appeal to the remedial power of the court. The defenses are not for the benefit of the defendant, but for the protection of the integrity of the court. The defenses based on plaintiff's conduct originally developed in equity. In courts of chancery, a plaintiff could appeal for fairness and equity only if he also conducted himself fairly. Thus, the ancient legal maxims provided that "he who comes in equity must do equity," and "that two wrongs don't make a right." The court refuses to be a mediator between two wrongdoers, for example, deciding the ownership of profits illegally stolen by two thieves. While the equitable defenses based on plaintiff's conduct initially arose in equity, the merger of law and equity now makes the defenses generally applicable to legal remedies in most, but not all, jurisdictions.

132.   **Answer (B) is the correct answer.** The facts do not suggest any applicable remedial defense because the plaintiffs' alleged misconduct of drinking is not related to the accident or the negligent driving of the truck driver.

   Answer (A) is incorrect. While some jurisdictions still restrict equitable defenses like unclean hands and laches to equitable claims, most apply the defenses equally to both claims at law and equity. Thus, the distinction between law and equity does not resolve the question here.

   Answer (C) is incorrect. While the merger of law and equity has made the remedial defenses applicable to all claims in most jurisdictions, that distinction does not resolve the question here. There is still no remedial defense applicable to the case.

   Answer (D) is incorrect. The passengers were not driving the car and thus are not potentially involved in the accident so as to negate the defendants' liability. Comparative fault is not a remedial defense, but rather a bar to liability when the plaintiff has engaged in misconduct equal to or greater than the defendant's actions causing the harm.

133.   **Answer (A) is the correct answer.** Laches relates to the delay of the plaintiffs in prosecuting the action.

   Answer (B) is incorrect because the statute of limitations is a legal remedy regarding the delay in commencing the action. The maxim relates to an equitable rather than a legal remedy.

   Answer (C) is incorrect because unclean hands concerns a plaintiff's misconduct rather than a delay or sleeping on one's rights.

   Answer (D) is incorrect. *In pari delicto* is a legal remedy related to the misconduct of the plaintiff that is equal to or greater than that of the defendant.

134. **Answer (D) is the correct answer.** Under the "American Rule," a prevailing party is not entitled to recover its attorney fees from the losing party. Rather, each party pays its own fees. An exception to the American Rule exists when a party acts in bad faith. However, generally, this exception applies only when a party acts in bad faith during its conduct of the litigation or when the party acts in bad faith in instituting the litigation. A party's conduct that gives rise to the substantive claim does not create liability for attorney fees. Thus, Simpson will not be liable for attorney fees based on Simpson's reasons for breaching the contract. **This result is found in Answer (D), making Answer (D) the correct answer and making Answers (A), (B) and (C) incorrect.**

135. **Answer (B) is the correct answer.** When a lawyer recovers a common fund that will benefit claimants other than the lawyer's own client, the lawyer is entitled to recover her reasonable attorney fees from the common fund. Here, the settlement fund will benefit all class members who were wrongfully denied reimbursement for the professional licensing fees. Thus, Pilot is entitled to recover attorney fees from the settlement fund under the common fund exception to the American Rule.

      Answer (A) is incorrect. A prevailing party is not entitled to recover her attorney fees automatically. Rather, she may recover them only if one of the exceptions to the "American Rule" applies.

      Answer (C) is incorrect. Even if a class member elects not to file a proof of claim and collect a portion of the settlement fund, the class member has received a benefit because the class member was entitled to present a claim and receive a portion of the fund if the class member so elected. *See Boeing Co. v. Van Gemert*, 444 U.S. 472 (1980).

      Answer (D) is incorrect. Under the common fund exception, the prevailing plaintiff can recover her reasonable attorney fees from the common fund even if the prevailing plaintiff herself benefits from the judgment as long other claimants will benefit as well.

136. **Answer (A) is the correct answer.** The federal Civil Rights Act permits a court to award a prevailing party its attorney fees. While the plain language of the statute gives the court discretion to award or withhold an award of fees to a prevailing party, the Supreme Court has recognized that a prevailing plaintiff in a civil rights case, and a Title VII case in particular, should "ordinarily" be awarded attorney fees. *See Christiansburg Garment Co. v. EEOC*, 434 U.S. 412 (1978); *Newman v. Piggie Park Enter.*, 390 U.S. 400 (1968).

      Answer (B) is incorrect. Attorney fees are awarded to the prevailing party in a Title VII case as a matter of course regardless of the theory upon which the plaintiff prevails.

Answer (C) is incorrect. Title VII statutorily provides for an award of attorney fees to a prevailing party. Thus, Plaintiff need not fit her case into the common law bad faith litigation exception to the American Rule. The Supreme Court has recognized that attorney fees should be awarded to a prevailing plaintiff in a civil rights case even if the defendant did not act in bad faith. *See Newman v. Piggie Park Enter.*, 390 U.S. 400 (1968).

Answer (D) is incorrect. A prevailing plaintiff in a civil rights case is entitled to attorney fees even if she recovered damages or monetary relief out of which her fees could otherwise be paid.

137. **Answer (D) is the correct answer.** Many federal civil rights statutes such as the ADA permit a prevailing plaintiff to recover her attorney fees. The Supreme Court has held that a party is a prevailing plaintiff if she receives some judicial relief on the merits of her claim and that judicial relief materially alters the legal relationship between the parties in a way that benefits the plaintiff. While voluntary settlement agreements are generally insufficient, the Court has recognized that settlement agreements enforced through judicially entered consent decrees may serve as the basis for an award of attorney fees. *See Buckhannon Board and Care Home v. West Virginia Dept. of Health and Human Resources*, 532 U.S. 598 (2001). Here, the settlement agreement has been incorporated into a judicially enforceable consent decree. By obligating Dressel to make wheelchair accommodations in one of its theaters, the consent decree alters the legal relationship between Dressel and Patterson in a way that benefits Patterson because Patterson will be able to access the theater after the wheelchair accommodations are made, and Dressel had no obligation to make the accommodations until the consent decree was entered.

Answer (A) is incorrect. A settlement agreement can serve as the basis of an award of attorney fees if it is incorporated into a judicially enforceable consent decree.

Answer (B) is incorrect. A plaintiff need not recover monetary relief to be considered a prevailing party. Equitable relief can serve as a basis for an award of attorney fees.

Answer (C) is incorrect. A plaintiff need not recover all of the relief that she seeks to be entitled to attorney fees. Instead, the plaintiff will be considered a prevailing party as long as she succeeds on any significant issue in the litigation and is awarded relief that achieves some of the benefit that she sought in bringing the suit. Here, the provision of wheelchair accommodations in one theater is some of the benefit Patterson sought in bringing the suit.

138. **Answer (B) is the correct answer.** A civil rights plaintiff who is a prevailing party is entitled to recover his reasonable attorney fees. Courts generally award attorney fees based on the "lodestar" method. Under the lodestar method, the court determines a reasonable hourly rate then multiplies that rate by the number of hours reasonably expended on the litigation. In determining the reasonableness of the fee award, the court may consider the degree of the plaintiff's overall success and reduce the award if the

plaintiff achieves only a limited success. Here, because Patterson succeed in altering only one of the fifteen theaters and received no damages, a court may reduce the attorney fees award.

Answer (A) is incorrect. A prevailing plaintiff is entitled to recover only a reasonable attorney fee.

Answer (C) is incorrect. In *Hensley v. Eckerhart*, 461 U.S. 424 (1983), the Supreme Court recognized that when a plaintiff's claims involve a common core of facts, it will be difficult to divide a lawyer's time on a claim-by-claim basis. In such circumstances, rather than attempting to divide the hours expended on a claim-by-claim basis, the court should focus on the reasonableness of the fees in light of the success obtained. Here, Patterson's claims pertaining to all of the theaters arise from a common core of facts such that much of the work performed by Patterson's counsel was likely devoted to the claims as a whole. As such, the court will award Patterson fees for all of the time expended but reduce the award to reflect Patterson's limited success.

Answer (D) is incorrect. The Supreme Court has recognized that the "technical" nature of the award does not affect whether the plaintiff is a prevailing party and, thus, is entitled to a fee award. Rather, the degree of success affects the reasonableness of the award. *See Farrar v. Hobby*, 506 U.S. 566 (1992). Further, Patterson's victory in this litigation is not technical or *de minimis*. While Patterson did not receive all of the relief sought, the alteration of one theater is a significant change in the relationship between Patterson and Dressel.

139. In determining the reasonableness of a fee award, a court will consider numerous factors, including the time and labor required to litigate the claims; the novelty of the claims and the difficulty of the issues raised in the suit; the skill required to prepare the case; the loss of other employment opportunities as a result of the case; the customary fee; time limitations imposed by the case or client; the success obtained; the expertise of the attorney; the "undesirability" of the case; the nature and length of the attorney-client relationship; and awards in similar cases.

140. **Answer (C) is the correct answer.** In *Marek v. Chesny*, 473 U.S. 1 (1985), the Supreme Court held that when a prevailing plaintiff in a civil rights action recovers less at trial than the plaintiff would have recovered under a valid offer of judgment, Federal Rule of Civil Procedure 68 precludes the prevailing plaintiff from recovering any *post-offer* attorney fees.

Answer (A) is incorrect. In *Marek*, the Supreme Court held that a defendant need not specify separately which portion of an offer of judgment is in satisfaction of costs and attorney fees.

Answer (B) is incorrect. In *Marek*, the Supreme Court held that a plaintiff could not combine post-offer costs with the judgment awarded at trial in determining whether the award at trial exceeded the offer of judgment.

Answer (D) is incorrect. In *Marek*, the Supreme Court recognized that a prevailing plaintiff who recovers less at trial than the plaintiff would have recovered under the offer of judgment is still a prevailing plaintiff and, hence, entitled to recover the plaintiff's *pre-offer* attorney fees.

PRACTICE FINAL EXAM: ANSWERS

141. **Answer (A) is the correct answer.** When a seller has wrongfully failed to deliver goods, UCC § 2-712 allows a buyer to "cover" by purchasing substitute goods and to recover from the seller as damages the difference between the cost of cover and the contract price. However, the buyer's failure to cover does not preclude the buyer from recovering damages. Instead, under the UCC § 2-713(a), a buyer is entitled to recover as damages the difference between the market price and the contract price. Here, Sally wrongfully failed to deliver her used car. Bradford has failed to cover. However, Bradford is entitled to recover damages under § 2-713(a). Bradford's damages will be measured as the difference between the market price of $2000 and the contract price of $1500. Thus, Bradford will be entitled to recover $500. This result is found in **Answer (A), making Answer (A) the correct answer** and **Answers (B), (C), and (D) incorrect answers.**

142. There are several advantages to seeking declaratory relief rather than an injunction. Both provide a preventive remedy that can avoid harm. Declarations however are easier to obtain because they do not require that irreparable injury or the inadequacy of damages be proven. Declaratory judgments are often placed on a shorter procedural timetable in court and thus a client can obtain relief more quickly. Declaratory judgments also have the strategic advantage of preserving ongoing business relations between parties because, unlike injunctions, they do not carry the threat of contempt. Declaratory judgments also provide for supplemental or further relief in the event that the defendant does not voluntarily comply with the court's determination of the appropriate legal rights.

143. **Answer (B) is the correct answer.** To recover damages for future expenses, an injured plaintiff must show that it is more likely than not that she will incur the future expenses. Here, because only a small number of people develop future vision problems and because Plaintiff has not shown any signs of developing future problems, Plaintiff will not be able to show that it is more likely than not that she will incur future medical expenses related to the treatment of any recurring vision problems. Hence, damages for Plaintiff's future medical expenses are too speculative.

Answer (A) is incorrect. Plaintiff will be able to recover the reasonable value of the surgery as long as she shows it was reasonably necessary. Because the surgery restored

157

her vision and posed only a small risk of complications, Plaintiff will be able to show that the surgery was reasonably necessary.

Answer (C) is incorrect. Under the collateral source rule, the payments from her employer are considered benefits that are collateral to the defendant. Thus, the defendant cannot offset these benefits against Plaintiff's harm.

Answer (D) is incorrect. Plaintiff cannot recover damages for medical expenses related to the treatment of future vision problems because Plaintiff cannot demonstrate that she more likely than not will suffer from future vision problems.

144. **Answer (D) is the correct answer.** Larry's own subjective fears, in the absence of any other conduct by Slime, are insufficient to establish a real threat of harm upon which the court can act. An injunction must be necessary to prevent harm, and no such threat of harm is shown here.

Answer (A) is incorrect because the facts do not demonstrate Slime's propensity to commit a legal harm. Slime's general reputation is insufficient to establish his propensity to commit the particular harm of failing to produce documents in this case.

Answer (B) is incorrect. While the scope of an injunction must match the scope of the harm, scope is a legal matter determined after the necessity of an injunction is established. The necessity of an injunction due to a real threat of imminent harm is not shown here.

Answer (C) is incorrect. Slime's failure to produce documents would constitute irreparable injury since damages would be insufficient to replace the loss of documents valuable to prosecuting and resolving the case. However, necessity of an injunction must be shown in addition to irreparable injury. For the reasons stated above regarding **Answers (B)** and **(C),** such legal necessity is not demonstrated here.

145. **Answer (A) is the correct answer.** Money damages were available at law as a remedy for breach of contract. Thus, a right to a jury trial will attach if Baker seeks money damages.

Answer (B) is incorrect. Although breach of contract was a claim recognized by common law courts, specific performance was available as a remedy only in equity. The right to a jury trial will not attach if either a claim was not cognizable at common law or the remedy sought was not available in common law courts. Because specific performance is an equitable remedy, no right to a jury trial attaches.

Answer (C) is incorrect. Only money damages will entitle Baker to a jury trial. Specific performance is an equitable remedy to which no right to a jury trial attaches.

Answer (D) is incorrect. Baker will be entitled to a jury trial if Baker seeks money damages.

146. **Answer (D) is the correct answer.** Courts generally will not order specific performance of personal service contracts because it would impose difficult burdens of supervision on the court to monitor the quality of the employment and the relationship with the employer. Thus, the burden on the court from enforcing this injunction and the public policy weighing in favor of free competition in the employment market weigh against the granting of specific performance. The general policy against specifically enforcing employment contracts and requiring personal servitude is implicated less in a case like this one where the employee, rather than the employer, seeks to enforce the contract.

Answer (A) is incorrect because detrimental reliance is irrelevant to the question asked and is not a basis for qualifying for an injunction.

Answer (B) is incorrect. Although Mr. Clean's contract is unique given the fact of a "once-in-a-lifetime" opportunity in a personalized, family business, the public policy against specific performance of employment contracts weighs against the issuance of the injunction.

Answer (C) is incorrect because the facts suggest that Mr. Clean cannot find another job as the contract is for a "once-in-a-lifetime" opportunity. If Mr. Clean were able to find another job, then the job would not be unique, and specific performance would be inappropriate.

147. An attorney for the successful plaintiffs would first seek preventive injunctive measures to stop the harm. Such preventive measures would order the state to stop sexually assaulting and harassing female inmates and to stop the cruel and unusual conditions of confinement. The plaintiffs would also seek to correct or reverse the existing conditions with reparative injunctive relief that would require the provision of adequate medical care, the establishment of sanitary conditions, and corrective action against the perpetrators of harassment. Due to the severity of the infractions and the personal invasions, the plaintiffs would also seek prophylactic measures designed to install preventive, cautionary steps that would aim to avert future harm. Such prophylactic measures could include the establishment of standards of care for the medical treatment, environmental standards for the temperature and cleanliness of the prison, policy measures against sexual harassment and assault, training and education of employees regarding sexual harassment, the establishment of a grievance process for inmates, and the development of employee sanctions for violations of the policy.

148. Porter's counsel has made a per diem argument. A per diem argument is a suggestion to the jury during closing argument that the jury calculate a plaintiff's pain and suffering damages by determining what amount of damages would be appropriate compensation for each day of pain and suffering then multiplying that amount by the number of days that the plaintiff will incur the pain and suffering. Many jurisdictions permit plaintiff's counsel to make such per diem arguments. However, some jurisdictions have rejected per diem arguments. Jurisdictions that reject per diem arguments do so on the ground that they are unduly prejudicial to defendants for several reasons. First, the per diem

figure suggested by counsel is not evidence, but rather argument of counsel. The per diem argument, thus, invites the jury to calculate damages based on argument rather than evidence. Second, the per diem argument unfairly assumes that pain is constant, uniform and continuous during the injured plaintiff's life. This may not be the case. Because of the reasons, the jury may be misled by the per diem argument. Defense counsel in the problem could raise an objection to the per diem argument by Porter's counsel on these grounds.

149. **Answer (D) is the correct answer.** Homeowner would prefer rescission to cancel the contract for the sale of the house and return to the pre-contact position by being reimbursed for the costs of moving and expert investigation. The seller's fraud and substantial breach of contract in delivering a non-habitable home is a sufficient basis for rescission.

Answer (A) is incorrect. The facts indicate that Homeowner is seeking a restitutionary remedy, but implied-in-fact contract is not a theory of restitution. The finding of an implied-in-fact contract establishes the existence of an actual contract upon which further legal or equitable relief can be awarded. Here, Homeowner does not seek compensation for losses in the amount of the diminution in market value of the home; instead, Homeowner wants to cancel the contract.

Answer (B) is incorrect. There is no need to imply a contract at law when an express contract exists between the parties for the sale of the house.

Answer (C) is incorrect. Quantum meruit is an implied-in-law contract for the value of services. Homeowner is not seeking monetary payment for any services, and thus quantum meruit is inapplicable here.

150. **Answer (D) is the correct answer.** For a preliminary injunction, the plaintiffs must show harm to themselves during the trial that cannot later be remedied with monetary damages. Here, the district court found that damages would be adequate, thus negating the existence of irreparable harm.

Answer (A) is incorrect because the court expressly held that the plaintiffs do not have a likelihood of success because the legal question is close.

Answer (B) is incorrect. Harm to the plaintiffs alone is insufficient to establish irreparable injury necessary for preliminary relief. Instead, the plaintiffs must show harm during the litigation that cannot later be addressed by monetary damages. As discussed above in **Answer (D),** that irreparable injury cannot be shown here.

Answer (C) is incorrect. Preliminary relief can be denied where the burden to the defendant is greater than the irreparable harm to the plaintiff. However, the facts given do not suggest any particular undue hardship to the city.

151.   **Answer (C) is the correct answer.** The court can award the attorney fees as a measure of civil compensatory contempt imposed after the civil hearing of which defendant had notice and an opportunity to appear.

   Answer (A) is incorrect because the determinate jail sentence is a criminal contempt penalty imposed for the attorney's past failure to appear without the full panoply of criminal procedural protections including the right to counsel, right against self-incrimination, and proof beyond a reasonable doubt.

   Answer (B) is incorrect because the fine would be a criminal contempt measure that could not be imposed in the absence of full criminal procedures.

   Answer (D) is incorrect because this is not a situation of frivolous conduct during litigation but rather a direct violation of a court's order to appear for trial.

152.   **Answer (A) is the correct answer.** To be liable for punitive damages, unlike liability for an intentional tort, a defendant must intend not only the conduct but also must intend to cause harm. Here, because the casino patron intended to touch the dealer, he may be liable for an intentional tort. However, because he was jubilant over a big win, the patron likely did not intend to cause harm to the dealer. Therefore, the patron would not be liable for punitive damages.

   Answer (B) is incorrect. Here, because the law student was disappointed with her grade, she likely intended to harm the professor and, thus, acted with the requisite bad state of mind. Additionally, because she caused serious physical injuries, her conduct rises to the requisite level of serious misconduct.

   Answer (C) is incorrect. Although punitive damages are not appropriate in contract cases, punitive damages may be awarded if the misconduct constituting a breach of contract also constitutes an independent tort. Here, if the repair person knowingly misrepresented the time required for performance to induce the customer to enter into the contract, the misrepresentation would constitute both a breach of contract and the independent tort of fraud. Fraudulent conduct will support an award of punitive damages.

   Answer (D) is incorrect. As discussed above, an award of punitive damages would not be appropriate in the case described in **Answer (A).**

153.   **Answer (C) is the correct answer.** To qualify for a constructive trust in many jurisdictions, a defendant's wrongdoing must involve a fraud or breach of some type of trust, confidence, or fiduciary duty. While Father has not fulfilled his promise of a gift to Daughter, he has not engaged in the type of fraud or breach of confidence which is the necessary predicate for a constructive trust.

   Answer (A) is incorrect. To qualify for a constructive trust in many jurisdictions, a defendant 1) must engage in wrongdoing that involves a breach of trust, and 2) plaintiff must have originally owned the property at issue. Both of these requirements are missing here where Father has always owned the business property and has not engaged in fraud or breach of confidence.

Answer (B) is incorrect. According to the facts, Daughter has not made any improvements to the Father's business property, nor has Daughter provided any other service or benefit to Father for which a debt would be owed.

Answer (D) is incorrect. Equitable lien is a restitution remedy that awards payment for a debt owed and secures that debt with the tangible property that is the subject of the dispute. Here, there is tangible property available with which to secure an equitable lien in the form of the Father's business property that is the basis of the dispute.

154.   **Answer (D) is the correct answer.** Generally, medical expenses between the time of injury and death, pain and suffering, and lost wages are all items of compensable damages in a survival action such as the one brought by Victor's Representative. However, most jurisdictions limit recovery for pain and suffering to recovery for only conscious pain and suffering. Here, because Victor never regained consciousness after his injury, he could have no conscious pain and suffering. Thus, his Estate will not be entitled to recover damages for pain and suffering. Additionally, most jurisdictions cut off recovery for lost wages at death. Thus, Victor's Estate will not be entitled to recover damages for lost wages over his entire natural worklife span. As such, Victor's Estate can recover damages only for the medical expenses Victor incurred between the time of injury and his death. **This result is found in Answer (D), making Answer (D) the correct answer and Answers (A), (B) and (C) incorrect.**

155.   **Answer (A) is the correct answer.** Most jurisdictions allow the next-of-kin of a decedent to maintain an action for wrongful death against the tortfeasor who caused the decedent's death. Additionally, most jurisdictions allow the next-of-kin to recover damages for both their economic and noneconomic losses. These damages include damages for loss of financial support and services provided by the decedent as well as the loss of the decedent's society and companionship. However, a few jurisdictions limit recovery to damages for the next-of-kin's economic losses only. Here, because Dan wrongfully caused Victor's death, Victor's Beneficiaries can maintain an action for wrongful death and recover damages both for their loss of financial support from Victor and their loss of his companionship. **This result is found in Answer (A), making Answer (A) the correct answer and Answers (B), (C) and (D) incorrect.**

156.   **Answer (C) is the correct answer.** If the seller does not resell the goods or resells the goods in a manner that does not conform with the UCC, the seller is not precluded from recovery. Instead, the seller may recover the difference between the contract price and the market price at the time and place for tender. Here, Sampson did not resell the trucks in accordance with the UCC. However, Sampson is not precluded from recovery. Instead, Sampson can recover the difference between the contract price of $7500 per truck and the market price of $7000 per truck, or $500 per truck.

Answer (A) is incorrect. A seller is not entitled to recover the purchase price from a breaching buyer unless (1) the buyer accepts the goods; (2) the goods are damaged after the risk of loss has passed to the buyer; or (3) the goods cannot be resold through reasonable efforts. Here, Bivens has not accepted the trucks, nor have the trucks been damaged. Further, Sampson was able to resell the trucks, suggesting that the trucks were not so unique that they could not be resold. Thus, Sampson is not entitled to recover the price.

Answer (B) is incorrect. When a buyer rejects conforming goods, UCC § 2-703 permits the seller to resell the goods and recover the difference between the contract price and the resale price. If the seller elects to resell the goods, the seller must do so in a commercially reasonable manner, and if the seller resells the goods at a private sale, the seller must give the breaching buyer notice of the seller's intent to resell the goods. Here, Sampson attempted to resell the trucks. However, Sampson resold the trucks at a private sale but failed to give Bivens notice of the resale. Moreover, the discrepancy between the market price of $7000 and the resale price of $3000 might indicate that Sampson did not sell the trucks in a commercially reasonable manner. Thus, Sampson cannot recover the difference between the contract price of $7500 per truck and the resale price of $3000 per truck, or $4500 per truck.

Answer (D) is incorrect. If a nonbreaching seller fails to resell the goods or resells the goods in a manner that does not conform with the UCC, the seller is not precluded from recovery. Instead, the seller may recover the difference between the contract price and the market price at the time and place for tender.

157. **Answer (B) is the correct answer.** There is no showing that the protestors have violated or are likely to violate any law. There was no past illegal behavior nor any planned action that in and of itself is illegal. The protestors have a right under the First Amendment to free speech.

Answer (A) is incorrect. The notice here was adequate as the police delivered a copy of the motion for temporary relief to the protest leaders. Even though actual notice is not required, it was obtained in this case upon personal delivery.

Answer (C) is incorrect. The imminence factor requiring close proximity in time of the alleged threat is satisfied here by the scheduled timing of the protest next week. It is not the timing, but rather the absence of a threatened harm that disqualifies the temporary injunction here.

Answer (D) is incorrect. *Ex parte* hearings in which only one party appears before the judge are constitutional under Due Process.

158. **Answer (B) is the correct answer.** Civil compensatory contempt is a monetary fine assessed to compensate a party for costs incurred as a result of the opposing party's violation of a court order. Here, the monetary award compensates Smith for the costs Smith incurred as a result of Clintex's violation of the court order. Civil contempt requires the opportunity to be heard, and the court provided that opportunity to Clintex.

Answer (A) is incorrect. The fine here for the past violation is not fixed as an arbitrary penalty, but instead is measured precisely by the amount of loss caused by the defendant.

Answer (C) is incorrect because the court provided the proper procedures of notice and an opportunity to be heard. The procedures are required as part of the process of awarding contempt, but are not necessarily required prior to the court's ruling.

Answer (D) is incorrect. The fine is not a criminal contempt remedy as discussed with respect to **Answer (A).** If it were criminal contempt, the procedures used by the court would be insufficient to sustain the award.

159. **Answer (B) is the correct answer.** Patterson is entitled to recover the cost to repair the car if repairs are both economically and physically feasible. Courts differ in the manner in which they measure economic feasibility. However, one measure is the pre-tort value of the car.

Answer (A) is incorrect. Repairs must be both physically and economically feasible.

Answer (C) is incorrect. Most courts reject the cost to repair when it exceeds either the diminution in value or the pre-tort value of the car regardless of the owner's reasons for repairing the car.

Answer (D) is incorrect. Patterson is entitled to recover the cost to repair the car as long as the repairs are physically and economically feasible. Economic feasibility will be measured by either the pre-tort value of the car or the diminution in value to the car as a result of the accident.

160. **Answer (D) is the correct answer.** There is an imminent threat to the testing company from the use of its secret testing questions within the next ten days that the court could prevent. In addition, the company would seek a preliminary injunction to bar the use of the test questions while the litigation is pending.

Answer (A) is incorrect because it is incomplete. The company can obtain a temporary injunction, but it can also seek preliminary relief.

Answer (B) is incorrect because it is incomplete. The company can obtain preliminary relief, but it can also request a temporary injunction.

Answer (C) is incorrect because a party cannot seek a permanent injunction until the completion of trial. Here, trial is not scheduled for eight more months and thus it is not the appropriate time to seek permanent relief.

161. Under UCC § 2-709 a seller is entitled to recover price for goods identified to the contract that the seller is unable to resell through reasonable efforts. Here, Super Tees completed 100 t-shirts that are identified to the contract with Beasely. Super Tees will be unable to resell the t-shirts because they commemorate Beasely's graduation. Thus, Super Tees will be entitled to recover the price of $400 ($4.00 per shirt × 100 completed

shirts). Super Tees also will be entitled to recover its lost profits for the remaining 100 t-shirts. UCC § 2-704 allows a seller that has not completed manufacture of the contract goods prior to the breach to cease manufacturing if to do so would be commercially reasonable. Here, Super Tees acted reasonably in ceasing production because no market appears to exist for the commemorative t-shirts. When a seller ceases production, market and resale differential damages will be inadequate. The measures envision the resale and the market price of finished goods. Thus, such a "components seller" is entitled to lost profits under § 2-708(2). Here, because Super Tees ceased production of the remaining 100 t-shirts, it has no finished goods. Accordingly, it is entitled to lost profits. Under UCC § 2-708(2), lost profits are measured as the seller's profits including reasonable overhead plus due allowance for costs reasonably incurred and less any payments or proceeds on resale. Profit is measured as the contract price less the seller's production costs. Here, Super Tee's anticipated profit was $2.50 per shirt or $250 (($4.00 contract price − $1.00 cost of shirt − $0.30 cost of ink − $.020 cost of overhead) × 100 shirts). Super Tees is entitled to recover $20 cost of overhead ($0.20 × 100 shirts). Super Tees also is entitled to recover costs it has reasonably incurred. Here, Super Tees already has paid $100 for the 100 t-shirts ($1.00 per shirt × 100 shirts) and $30 for the ink ($0.30 per shirt × 100 shirts). Assuming, Super Tees acted reasonably in purchasing the blank t-shirts and ink, it will be entitled to recover these costs as well. Super Tees' recovery will be reduced by any proceeds it received on resale of the components. Here, Super Tees was able to sell the blank t-shirts for $50 ($0.50 per shirt × 100 shirts). Finally, Super Tees is entitled to recover any incidental damages it incurred in mitigating its loss. Here, Super Tees had to pay $10 ($0.10 per shirt × 100 shirts) to ship the blank t-shirts to the new purchaser. Thus, Super Tees' recovery will be $760 ($400 (price for completed t-shirts) + $250 (profit on unfinished t-shirts) + $20 (overhead attributable to unfinished t-shirts) + $130 (costs incurred for blank t-shirts and ink) − $50 (profit earned on resale of blank t-shirts) + $10 (incidental damages for shipping blank t-shirts)). This result is found in **Answer (B), making Answer (B) the correct answer and Answers (A), (C) and (D) incorrect answers.**

162. **Answer (B) is the correct answer.** Generally, the trier of fact determines whether to impose punitive damages and in what amount. Thus, if a jury is the trier of the fact, the jury determines whether and in what amount to impose punitive damages. Further, the imposition of punitive damages is always discretionary. Even if the jury determines that the defendant acted with the requisite state of mind to be liable for punitive damages, the jury in its discretion may choose not to impose punitive damages on the defendant. Thus, here, even if the jury determines that Davidson acted intentionally and, thus, could be liable for punitive damages, the jury may, but need not, impose punitive damages.

Answer (A) is incorrect. The imposition of punitive damages is always discretionary. The jury is never required to impose punitive damages.

Answer (C) is incorrect. Generally, the trier of fact determines whether to impose punitive damages and in what amount. Thus, if a jury is the trier of the fact, the jury determines whether and in what amount to impose punitive damages.

Answer (D) is incorrect. If Davidson acted intentionally, punitive damages would be appropriate.

163. **Answer (A) is the correct answer.** The defendant Billy may assert the defense of waiver arguing that Bobby unilaterally relinquished his right to sue for breach of contract by going through with the sale even though his roommate told him of the lack of value in the cards. His father's statement establishes knowledge on Bobby's part regarding his right to a contract as warranted.

      Answer (B) is incorrect. Estoppel would be a defense barring Bobby from changing legal positions regarding the validity of the contract. He first acceded to the value of the contract despite the knowledge from this father, but now seeks to change that position. However, estoppel requires detrimental reliance on the part of Billy, and there are no facts to establish such detrimental reliance.

      Answer (C) is incorrect because estoppel is not a valid defense as explained in **Answer B** above.

      Answer (D) is incorrect because the unconscionability defense is not available to Billy, but rather may be a defense for *Bobby* to consider. Unconscionability is a defense regarding oppressiveness in the creation or content of the contract. The defense would likely fail even as raised by Bobby because his roommate provided the notice and counsel necessary to counter any unfair bargaining power.

164. By excluding evidence of cost-of-living increases to wages but using a market discount rate, Judge Grumpy treated inflation inconsistently. Judge Grumpy refused to recognize that Plaintiff's future earnings would increase due to inflation. However, because a market interest rate reflects anticipated inflation, Judge Grumpy reduced her present award on the theory that she would earn more on her investment over time based on inflation. As such, Plaintiff may be undercompensated.

165. **Answer (B) is the correct answer.** Courts will issue injunctions where the irreparable injury to the plaintiff outweighs any undue hardship to the defendant. Here, the serious physical and emotional harm to Mrs. Small is intangible harm that cannot adequately be remedied after the fact with damages. While damages could be computed for her harm, the public policy preference is to avoid physical harm to individuals by preventing its occurrence. While Big, Bad and Boom may have some undue hardship in the form of financial loss from relocation or adaptation of its manufacturing process, that hardship does not outweigh the harm to the plaintiff.

      Answer (A) is incorrect. Significant economic waste to a defendant is a basis upon which a court may deny the plaintiff its injunction. The facts here are close to the line of establishing undue hardship in possibly requiring Big, Bad, and Boom to go out of business. However, it is also likely that the injunction will merely impose some financial costs upon Big, Bad and Boom as it relocates or adapts its manufacturing process to avoid pollution. The possible economic waste does not rise to the level courts have required in cases of physical and medical harm to people.

Answer (C) is incorrect. The public interest is one factor relevant to the court's balancing test for an injunction. However, there is no absolute policy in favor of commercial interests, especially where they interfere with individual rights, as in this case.

Answer (D) is incorrect because the plaintiff's desire for an injunction, standing alone, is insufficient basis on which to award an injunction.

166. **Answer (B) is the correct answer.** The case presents a definite, adverse, ripe controversy that is not altered by the plaintiff's request for a declaration rather than an injunction. *See Nashville v. Wallace*, 288 U.S. 249 (1933) (the classic case on state power to issue declaratory judgments).

Answer (A) is incorrect because there is an actual controversy. In addition, the language of "case or controversy" indicates a conclusion about the related, but distinct, concept of constitutional judicial power rather than the required threshold for declaratory judgments.

Answer (C) is incorrect because the claimant does not seek an advisory opinion that is hypothetical, but instead challenges a specific tax law and its application to the company.

Answer (D) is incorrect because if the legal question were hypothetical, the court would not have judicial power to issue declaratory relief.

167. **Answer (D) is the correct answer.** An accounting of profits would be a proper restitutionary remedy to address the unjust benefit gained by Big Films in appropriating the writer's story for its film. An accounting of profits remedy is measured by the amount of profit derived by the defendant from the wrong. The accounting measure offsets the total revenues made by the defendant ($65 million) with production costs ($5 million) and any profits related to the defendant's own efforts ($30 million from star Devine).

Answer (A) is incorrect. This is a measure of the plaintiff's loss, the payment she would have received from Big Films but for the wrong. However, restitution disgorges the defendant's gain, which is often greater than plaintiff's loss.

Answer (B) is incorrect. The $65 million in total revenues made by the defendant is the measure of an accounting remedy only where the defendant fails to show offsetting costs or disassociated profits. Here, Big Films has established an offset of $35 million from the production costs and profits associated with the star power of Devine.

Answer (C) is incorrect. The $60 million offsets the total revenues made by defendants minus its production costs. However, it fails to subtract out the amount of profits made by the defendants' own efforts of securing a famous star.

168.   **Answer (D) is the correct answer.** Because the land cannot be restored to productive agricultural use, the damage to the land is permanent. When damage to land is permanent, the landowner is entitled to recover the diminution in value to the land as a result of the damage.

Answer (A) is incorrect. Farmer Brown will not be entitled to recover the cost to remove the chemicals because the damage is permanent. The chemicals are not harmful to humans. Thus, the only use the chemicals prevent is an agricultural use. Removing the chemicals will not restore the land to agricultural use.

Answer (B) is incorrect. The damage to the land is permanent rather than temporary because removing the chemicals will not restore the land for agricultural use. Because the damage is permanent, Farmer Brown is not entitled to recover the cost to restore the land.

Answer (C) is incorrect. Even though the land is permanently damaged, Farmer Brown is not entitled to recover the full pre-contamination market value of the land because the land retains some productive uses after the contamination and, hence, retains some market value.

169.   **Answer (A) is the correct answer.** Farmer Brown is entitled to recover the lost profits on the crops as measured by the market value of the lost crops less the expenses saved in growing and harvesting the crops.

Answer (B) is incorrect. Awarding the full market value of the crops would overcompensate Farmer Brown because Farmer Brown has been saved the expense of growing and harvesting the crops.

Answer (C) is incorrect. The damage to the land and the damage to the crops are two distinct injuries. Thus, Farmer Brown can recover for both.

Answer (D) is incorrect. Farmer Brown can recover for lost crops as long as Farmer Brown can provide a reasonable basis for estimating the amount of crops lost and the value of those crops.

170.   **Answer (A) is the correct answer** because the court correctly sought to coerce future compliance with the injunction by assessing a daily fine which the defendants could avoid or purge by compliance with the order. *See Int'l Workers Union v. Bagwell*, 512 U.S. 821 (1994).

Answer (B) is incorrect because the order is structured as a valid coercive contempt remedy as indicated above, and the court provided the required process of notice and an opportunity to be heard.

Answer (C) is incorrect because a criminal contempt remedy would have been a fixed fine of a set amount for past violations that could not be avoided by defendants, rather than the indeterminate designation of a future, per day amount.

Answer (D) is incorrect because it does not describe what the court attempted to do here. The answer would have fit if the court had attempted a criminal contempt remedy to punish the defendants for a past violation, but failed to use sufficient criminal procedures mandated by the U.S. Constitution such as trial by jury, proof beyond a reasonable doubt, the right to counsel, and the right against self-incrimination.

171. In *State Farm v. Campbell*, 538 U.S. 408 (2003), the Supreme Court recognized that a punitive award that was more than 9 times greater than the compensatory award such as the award in this case was constitutionally suspect. However, the Court refused to create a bright line rule prohibiting such awards and recognized that such awards might be merited in some cases. Here, Plimpton could argue that a large punitive award was necessary to deter Big Brother because Big Brother was aware of previous similar misconduct and took no steps to prevent it. Likewise, Plimpton could argue that a large punitive award was necessary because Big Brother's conduct, while reprehensible, caused little economic harm. As such, a large punitive award was necessary to provide an incentive for victims to bring suit against Big Brother and, hence, to deter the misconduct. Big Brother could argue that such a large award is unjustified in this case because it is duplicative of the plaintiff's compensatory award. As in *State Farm*, the compensatory award here is sizeable and the bulk of the award is to compensate for non-economic losses such as emotional distress. In *State Farm*, the Court recognized that under such circumstances, much of the emotional distress for which the plaintiff is compensated is caused by the outrage and humiliation that the plaintiff suffered as a result of the defendant's action. Punitive damages also are imposed to condemn the defendant for causing such outrage and humiliation. In such cases, then, the compensatory award already contains a punitive element.

172. Laches and the statute of limitations both relate to delay in the plaintiff's pursuit of a remedy through litigation. Laches originated as an equitable defense and includes any delay during the course of litigation. The statute of limitations is a statutorily created defense that pertains only to the delay in initially commencing the action. In addition, laches requires prejudice to the defendant, whereas the statute of limitations is an absolute time bar regardless of the impact or lack of harm to the defendant. Finally, the statue of limitations prescribes a specific time in which an action has to be commenced whereas laches is flexible and focuses on the unreasonableness of the plaintiff's delay.

173. **Answer (C) is the correct answer.** Fashion Mavens' substantial breach of refusing to pay royalties for the use of the software as agreed in the contract is a sufficient basis upon which to seek rescission of the contract.

Answer (A) is incorrect. Proof of the inadequacy of legal damages is a required element in seeking equitable remedies. Rescission developed in both law and equity and thus inadequacy is not always required to qualify for relief. Moreover, an independent basis to qualify for the rescission remedy is first required (substantial breach, mistake, fraud, emergency) prior to consideration of whether rescission is an appropriate remedy over damages.

Answer (B) is incorrect. Mistake, either bilateral or unilateral known to the other side, can constitute a legal basis for rescission. However, the facts do not indicate that the failure to pay the royalties was a result of mistake.

Answer (D) is incorrect. If a court were to imply a contract at law, it would be using the restitutionary remedy of quasi-contract to award a restitution remedy. Quasi-contract is a separate restitutionary remedy distinct from rescission, and thus does not constitute a legal basis upon which to seek rescission.

174. **Answer (C) is the correct answer.** The measure of restitution for rescission seeks to return both parties to the status quo ante, the position they were in prior to the contract. To restore Software to its original position, it must disgorge the $60,000 received under the contract. To restore Fashion Mavens to its position, it must return the profits obtained by use of the software purchased under the contract. However, the law apportions the profits to require the return only of the profits obtained unjustly under the contract. The amount of profits Fashion Maven earned by its own efforts of marketing and consulting are not disgorged. *See, e.g., Earthinfo Inc. v. Hydrosphere Resource Consultants*, 900 P.2d 113 (Colo. 1995).

    Answer (A) is incorrect. Fashion Mavens does not have to disgorge the entire amount of its profits, but only the portion of the profits obtained unjustly by the use of software now required to be "returned" under the rescinded contract.

    Answer (B) is incorrect. While this answer correctly describes the apportionment of profits, it fails to return Software to its original position by requiring the offsetting disgorgement of the return of the initial contract payment.

    Answer (D) is incorrect. Monetary remedies measured by the amount of a plaintiff's loss are not restitution measures, but rather are measures of compensatory damages. Since Software is not seeking damages, this is an incorrect measure for restitution.

175. **Answer (B) is the correct answer.** If Insured prevails on either the bad faith or the breach of contract claim, Insured will be entitled to recover the attorney fees incurred in the client litigation as compensatory damages because the attorney fees were what Insured bargained for under the insurance contract and lost when Massive Mutual refused to defend client's lawsuit.

    Answer (A) is incorrect. If Insured prevails on the breach of contract claim only, he will be entitled to recover only those attorney fees he incurred in defending client's lawsuit because those were the attorney fees that he was promised under the insurance contract. Like any other attorney fees incurred in vindicating a party's contract rights, the attorney fees incurred in prosecuting the claims against Massive Mutual will be governed by the American Rule. Note that if Insured had prevailed on the bad faith claim as well as the breach of contract claim, many jurisdictions would allow Insured to recover all of his attorney fees, including those incurred in prosecuting the bad faith claim.

Answer (C) is incorrect. The attorney fees that Insured incurs in bringing his breach of contract action against Massive Mutual are like the attorney fees incurred by any other party that brings a breach of contract action. Under the American Rule, such attorney fees are not recoverable unless the insurance contract expressly provides for recovery of attorney fees. However, if Insured had prevailed on the bad faith claim as well as the breach of contract claim, many jurisdictions would allow Insured to recover all of his attorney fees, including those incurred in prosecuting the bad faith claim, as an exception to the American Rule.

Answer (D) is incorrect. Insured is entitled to recover the attorney fees he incurred in defending against client's claim.

176. **Answer (D) is the correct answer.** An equitable lien is an appropriate restitutionary remedy when a third party has made improvements to the property of another. The amount of debt owed to the church would be measured by the benefit gained by the Landlord in the amount of financial and construction investments into the building.

Answer (A) is incorrect. Constructive trust is generally not available as a remedy when the defendant has not engaged in a fraud or breach of confidence and where the property at issue was not originally owned by the plaintiff. Both of these predicate requirements are absent in this scenario.

Answer (B) is incorrect. An accounting of profits disgorges the profits gained by the defendant from its wrongdoing. Here, Landlord has not engaged in an illegal act or wrongdoing, but merely has retained the benefit conferred by the church on the assumption that it would be the eventual owner of the building.

Answer (C) is incorrect. Quantum meruit is not an equitable restitution theory, but instead is a legal device.

177. Most jurisdictions recognize an implied condition in every attorney-client contract that allows a client to discharge her attorney at any time with or without cause. Thus, Parker has not breached the retainer agreement by discharging Anderson. However, most jurisdictions also allow an attorney to recover the reasonable value of her services in quantum meruit when a client discharges the attorney before completion of the representation. In some jurisdictions, this right to quantum meruit is subject to two conditions. First, if the retainer agreement conditions the attorney's right to receive a fee on some condition such as the client's recovery, then the attorney has no right to quantum meruit recovery unless and until that contingency occurs. Second, an attorney cannot recover more in quantum meruit than she would have recovered under the retainer agreement. Here, the retainer agreement between Parker and Anderson

conditioned Anderson's right to receive a fee on Parker's obtaining a judgment or settlement. That contingency has occurred because Baker settled the case for Parker. Thus, Anderson is entitled to recover the reasonable value of services rendered to Parker. However, Anderson's recovery may be capped at $165,000 or 33% of the $500,000 settlement because that is the amount to which Anderson would have been entitled had the retainer agreement been performed.

178. **Answer (D) is the correct answer** because the moving party is attempting to use declaratory relief for the tactical advantage of evading the applicable time limits.

Answer (A) is incorrect because a declaration about the relative rights of the two parties with respect to the particular building permit at issue would terminate the uncertainty between those parties.

Answer (B) is incorrect because the controversy is ripe as the building permit has been denied and thus there are no further actions or facts which must occur before it would be the right time for the court to intervene in the dispute.

Answer (C) is incorrect because the Contractor presents a definite and concrete issue regarding its particular building permit and the actual reasons for denial.

179. **Answer (A) is the correct answer.** Unclean hands prohibits a plaintiff from coming into court to request equitable relief when it has engaged in misconduct. The misconduct must connect generally to the facts of the case, but not necessarily be directly related to the underlying claim. The plaintiff's misrepresentation in naming its product is related to the underlying trademark dispute sufficiently to bar it from seeking a remedy. A court will not adjudicate a dispute between two wrongdoers.

Answer (B) is incorrect. Defendant is being sued for trademark infringement. Any other potential liability of the defendant is not relevant to the availability of remedial defenses between the parties in this case.

Answer (C) is incorrect. The *defendant's* misconduct is not relevant to the plaintiff's claim for relief in this case. The defendant's misconduct could be relevant, under different circumstances, as a response to a counter-defense of the plaintiff or as a defense for the plaintiff against a counter-claim of the defendant.

Answer (D) is incorrect. *In pari delicto* would bar Big Fig's claim if it was at equal fault in the underlying trademark infringement at issue in the case.

180. **Answer (D) is correct.** In *Alyeska Pipeline Service Co. v. Wilderness Society*, 421 U.S. 240 (1975), the Supreme Court refused to recognize a public policy exception to the American Rule. Instead, the Court held that a prevailing party can recover its attorney fees only if the case fits into one of the pre-existing common law exceptions to the American Rule, including the common fund doctrine. However, the Court also recognized that the common fund exception does not apply when the plaintiff realizes only a generalized social benefit. Instead, the plaintiff's case must generate a common

fund to which an easily identified class of claimants has an undisputed and ascertainable claim. Here, Do-Right's claim raises important public policy issues, and the resolution of Do-Right's claims will affect future permit applications. However, under *Alyeska*, these are merely generalized social benefits that do not create a determinative common fund to which an indentifiable class of claimants has an ascertainable claim. Thus, Do-Right is not entitled to recover his attorney fees. **This result is found in Answer (D), making Answer (D) the correct answer and Answers (A), (B) and (C) incorrect.**

181.   **Answer (C) is the correct answer.** When a seller delivers non-conforming goods, the buyer is entitled to recover the difference between the value of the goods as accepted and the value of the goods had the goods been delivered in the condition warranted by the seller under UCC § 2-714. Under UCC § 2-715, a buyer also can recover consequential damages such as lost profits, if those losses were foreseeable and unavoidable. Under the UCC, consequential damages are foreseeable when the seller had reason to know of the particular needs of buyer that caused the consequential loss at the time of contracting. The UCC also requires the buyer to take reasonable steps through cover or otherwise to prevent the loss. If the loss occurs despite the buyer's reasonable efforts, the buyer can recover damages for the loss. Here, Specialty Products delivered a non-conforming press. Thus, Manufacturer is entitled to recover the difference between the value of the press as delivered and the value of the press as contracted for. At the time of contracting, Manufacturer informed Specialty Products that it needed the press to manufacture widgets that it intended to sell. Thus, Manufacturer's lost profits from the sale of widgets were foreseeable to Specialty Products. Finally, Manufacturer took prompt steps to repair the press. Thus, Manufacturer is entitled to recover its lost profits as well as the difference in value damages. This result is found in **Answer (C), making Answer (C) the correct answer and Answers (A), (B) and (D) incorrect answers.**

182.   **Answer (D) is the correct answer.** Damages are adequate here to replace Surfer Dude's loss. Where a legal remedy is adequate to return the plaintiff to his rightful position, the equitable remedy will be denied. Damages here will be measured by the difference in the contract price minus the market price of the wax ($6.00 – $5.00 = $1.00 × 100 cans = $100).

Answer (A) is incorrect because the surfer wax is not unique, as demonstrated by the market availability of a second brand of wax. The plaintiff's personal preference for a good, standing alone, is insufficient to establish the uniqueness or lack of fungibility of the good.

Answer (B) is incorrect because the additional cost of the replacement goods is relevant to the calculation of damages, and does not dictate the availability of equitable relief.

Answer (C) is incorrect because the contract for the sale of specified goods does not impose any additional burden of supervision or monitoring on the court. Where such a burden on the court does exist, courts will deny specific performance.

183. **Answer (C) is the correct answer.** Modification of the injunction is appropriate due to the changed factual circumstances of Joe's continued violation of the order. Prophylactic relief which goes beyond the legal harm to address the facilitators of harm is appropriate where the defendant has exhibited a history of similar illegal conduct. The order to stay 25 feet away from the castle is a prophylactic measure designed to provide an additional precaution against Joe's continued violation of Princess' privacy.

Answer (A) is incorrect because Joe's failure to comply with the prior injunction is a significant change in circumstances since the time of the prior order.

Answer (B) is incorrect because factually, Joe did not comply with the order in substance or in good faith. Additionally, the existence of a defendant's good faith compliance is a basis for seeking termination, rather than modification, of injunctive relief.

Answer (D) is incorrect because the modification would be too broad in scope by going beyond the harm or the contributors of that harm and unduly burdening Joe's First Amendment right to report the news on public figures like Princess. Modification of the prior injunction is appropriate, but that modification must be tailored to the scope of the changed circumstances.

184. Potter has two possible claims against Tyson. First, Potter can pursue the legal theory of conversion because Tyson stole the painting. Under this theory, Potter will be entitled to recover the $5000 fair market value of the painting at the time of conversion. Second, Potter can pursue the restitutionary theory of "waiver of the tort and suit in assumpsit." This theory implies a fictitious agency relationship between Potter and Tyson such that Tyson would be deemed to hold the painting for Potter's benefit and to have sold the painting on Potter's behalf. Under this theory, Potter would be entitled to recover the $1 million that Tyson received from the sale of the painting. In this case, Potter would want to waive the tort and sue in assumpsit because this theory would yield a greater recovery for Potter.

INDEX